The New Individualism

Personal Change to
Transform Society

Richard Botelho

Windstream Publishing Company
Danville, California

FIRST EDITION

All rights reserved, including the right of
reproduction in whole or in part in any form.

Copyright © 1994 by Richard Botelho

Published by Windstream Publishing Company
303 Windstream Place, Danville, CA 94526

Manufactured in the United States of America
ISBN: 0-9643926-1-5

Library of Congress Catalog Card No.: 94-61735

0 9 8 7 6 5 4 3 2 1

*To Sue Anne Eccleston,
and to people with hearts like hers
all over the world.*

Disclaimer

This publication is intended to provide a general framework for personal change as it relates to sociological condition, and is sold with the understanding that the publisher is not offering any professional services. Moreover, this publication is not meant to provide expert assistance with respect to personal development; in such cases, qualified professionals should be sought.

Contents

Acknowledgments vii
1. The Environment 1
2. Fear 18
3. Disillusionment 40
4. Understanding 55
5. Excitement 72
6. Morality 87
7. Power 111
8. Synthesis 128

Acknowledgments

I wish to thank the following people for their contribution to the formulation of *The New Individualism*, most of which occurred in conversations on how the world situation might be improved: Sue Anne Eccleston, Jim Riding, Mike Clemons, Eric Jacobson, Brad Boldrini and my Mom and Dad.

I also wish to thank Dr. Richard Hughes of California State University, Sacramento for his theoretical worldview and to Dr. George Tokmakoff, also of California State University, Sacramento for teaching me discipline and the value of inspiration.

Finally, I wish to thank Rick Martin of The Executive Committee (TEC) for his input and his intellectual example as well as all of the members of TEC 915 for their patience, guidance and vision.

The New Individualism

1
The Environment

We need to believe in people, for we have an incredible ability to know when something isn't working, whether that be our bodies or our spirits or our relations with the rest of humanity. For a time, most of us have been at least subliminally aware that there is a breakdown occurring in the system of which we are an integral part and we also know that we feel an underlying sense of disconnectedness and disconcertedness in what we see as a failure for ourselves and the society in which we live to exist harmoniously. Our awareness of the disjointed nature between ourselves and the larger whole despairs us since we know that if the system is faulty, then we as clay molded by the system must be flawed as well. We also understand that we are fundamentally a product of our environment and that culture does indeed shape and mold us, and so we further recognize that whatever actions we might take to improve our condition must be of a magnitude that is capable of changing our milieu.

At the core, we are troubled and anxious since we are unsure as to exactly what is causing our apprehension. Our incongruence is especially disturbing since we, as people, naturally seek answers as a by-product of our ability to think and reason, and our inability to fully understand the forces contributing to our confusion causes trepidation. Our "unknowing" is constant and this lack of clarity eats at us and is a continuous source of self-doubt and self-recrimination.

We are, however, biologically programed to survive as the self-preservation instinct is probably the strongest and most fundamental drive we have, and so we naturally seek to reconcile the incongruity between ourselves and our society in order to provide a state of security in which we can hopefully feel comfortable and safe. When, however, we are unable to formulate solutions, we do our best to suppress the source of our anxiety; this suppression blunts the search for solutions, the search itself containing the seeds of a curative plant. As a result, we are left disharmonious, using energy and even vitality, to maintain the suppression; this discordance is deleterious to the individual for it deprives him/her of much needed strength and desire.

A society follows essentially the same dynamic as that of the singular individual; the failure to manage deficiencies and to allow them to exist without resolution saps the culture of energy and requires tremendous amounts of expenditures in the form of both resources and time. For a society, this can mean billions of dollars of unnecessary outlays, a sapping of national spirit and pride, the gradual destruction of the environment, and the meaningless pursuit of "national" objectives which lack a true support base. For people within that society, this can mean disinterest and a general demotivation regarding their participation in a system that they increasingly perceive to be resistant to, or incapable of, constructive change; as a result, people naturally believe that their efforts are futile and thus a waste of time. The net result is an erosive complacency that portends more difficult times ahead for both people and their system.

Clearly, for both individuals and groups it is possible for a general malaise to result where a distinct lack of passion, drive, interest, purpose and meaning exist in the society. When we examine the current state of the world, particularly America, there can be no question that this apathy does exist and that as a by-product of this apathy a general uneasiness has engulfed our culture and threatens our vitality and commitment toward building a more promising future. But how did this malaise come about? What caused it?

An Incongruent System

During the past few decades, we as a nation have endured much; a substantial portion of our history during this period has been the story of successive disappointments that have led to a kind of aggregate disillusionment as our society witnessed unsatisfactorily explained assassinations, immoral wars, political scandals, economic mismanagement, and a gradual erosion of our educational system in which we once had so much pride. In combination, the above has led to a severe loss of our national spirit. Through the years, we have become aware of the dysfunction in our culture and this awareness has caused us to doubt our own abilities.

Of course, there have been some extremely rewarding cultural accomplishments as well, but in general there has been a national sense of "losing it" inasmuch as our experiences have fallen short of our expectations. We are also increasingly aware that our leadership position is now being challenged by many global competitors even though we have "won" the Cold War and should stand to reap the benefits of our victory. This relative diffusion of our power is very alarming to us as any fall from global preeminence naturally causes national self-doubt and a legitimate concern for the future prospects of the nation. Typically, there is a longing for the past and predictably our country has exhibited exactly the kind of nostalgia that is so characteristic of a nation that recognizes that the glory days have probably passed and that the future will probably not be as bright.

The rhetoric of our politicians who speak of greater days to come sounds hollow, and we don't really believe the "talk" anymore. We have heard it too many times before, and we know that

THE NEW INDIVIDUALISM

we have been deceived and lied to repeatedly. Our national consciousness appears to be one of resignation, and there also appears to be relatively little hope of a national resilience. Moreover, we are not even sure where to put what hope remains. We have tried so many different approaches already, and it seems that the road we are on meanders aimlessly and leads only to further complexity and confusion.

Our institutions, from government to church, have failed to provide whatever it is that we feel we need in order to be happy, and our sociological decay, as reported in our daily media, is proof that our deepest suspicions regarding our cultural deterioration are being validated. We have looked so longingly for answers and experienced so many disappointments that generally we look no more.

Our last collective attempt to provide hope for ourselves was really the me-generation experience fashioned in the 1960s and the 1970s. This was essentially an individually inspired attempt to seek shelter from the harsh reality of a general institutional and cultural collapse by retreating into the self; unfortunately, what this movement accomplished was a widespread cult of narcissism in which people became convinced that self-absorption and even greed were all that mattered. As it failed, people and the institutions of our society progressively decayed into an eventual moral and spiritual quagmire.

The retreat into oneself ultimately turned into forms of alienation, powerlessness, insecurity, and in extreme cases, isolation. But since humankind is a social animal, as John Donne noted centuries ago when he said that "no man is an island, entire of himself," our isolation cut us off from the very source of our potential resuscitation: the human family. As a result, the me-generation experience was doomed to fail since it was antithetical to one of humanity's most fundamental drives: the desire for social interaction, even social cause, and the bonded companionship that results from this process. What we have learned is that to turn inward as a defense against sociological dysfunction offers little hope for people and holds no promise as a remedy of societal misfortune since only people dedicated toward their own social cause can positively effect change on the system and on themselves.

The pervasive loneliness and corresponding lack of fulfillment of the me-generation period gave rise to the return of conservatism with a stated emphasis on family values and traditional morality; this occurred not so much out of promise, but rather out of default. The 1980s is really this story.

Unfortunately, the return to conservatism could not succeed since the version put forward was the same old dog with a new collar and people saw through the facade. Quite frankly, the world has become far too complex for traditional conservatism to provide any real answers since it fails to address the dramatically changing needs of a population which can no longer afford a stationary perspective.

With people unable to seek solutions through the various government and social institutions in our society, as well as a retreat into the self, what remained? Where does someone go for answers when the perceived sociological sources for explanations are exhausted? What do you do, either as an individual or a nation, when what remains of your search and its prospects for tomorrow are not exactly intolerable, but not exactly hopeful either?

The Absent Self-Corrective Mechanism

More than anything else, what really troubles our society is the lack of a self-corrective mechanism. We are deeply disturbed that our society and its institutions are not being sufficiently forwarded since this goes against our national grain to quickly identify a problem and provide a solution. The problems that face our nation and the world are being allowed to fester, which is especially upsetting since we know that our inattentiveness and lack of focus will only accelerate the rate of sociological decline. We know that social procrastination ultimately leads to a collapse of the system and of everything that we have built and striven for. Most troubling is that we do not know how to develop a self-corrective mechanism since our governmental and sociological institutions have generally tended to reinforce our reluctance to assume complete responsibility. Our sociological conditioning has relegated us to virtual subservience, instilling in us a belief that the scope of the "system" is beyond any individual's ability to change it. We have been conditioned to believe in the superiority of others, presumably those in the power positions, and if they cannot provide solutions then who are we to try. We have been "externally directed" and yet we know that the external is not working.

We had high hopes for science, but the failure of technology to remedy our social ills is well known and becoming increasingly notorious. Part of this "scientific hope" centered on human development, the so-called "self-help" movement, and while it is true that self-help literature and personal improvement seminars have been widely available for individuals, they have been conspicuously absent for society at large. In addition, self-help vehicles are generally underutilized by the majority of Americans and this serves to limit their collective utility because this underutilization precludes the development of a point of critical mass which might, at least potentially, cause pervasive and beneficial social change.

Where the lack of a self-corrective mechanism has been most conspicuously absent, however, is in our political system; the hope that government could somehow correct sociological malfunctions has been largely discredited as it became increasingly evident that government has proved woefully inadequate through its failure to eliminate large pockets of poverty, ease racial tensions, exercise sound fiscal management, or generally provide a more promising future for our children. Moreover, the electoral process has turned into a largely irrelevant circus of personal power grabbing and through its format failed to deliver substantive agendas and policies which could help the nation. After virtually every election, the electorate is left with the feeling that nothing will ultimately change and that the plight of the average citizen will only worsen over time.

Part of the reason for the relative lack of discussion concerning the issues is that neither of the two major political parties have any viable solutions to the problems of our nation, and both have accepted a relative powerlessness in the pursuit of their duties. The final year of the Bush administration, in which the government's ability to manage the economy was almost completely capitulated in deference to market forces, is but one example of how even the highest levels of American political leadership have abdicated their responsibilities. On some level, the American people understand this political dysfunction and this no doubt contributes to an alarming sense of despair and powerlessness among our citizenry. There is much acrimony against the political process itself, and we know that we must remove the bitterness and distrust if we are to reestablish trust and credibility within government. We also know, however, that this will be an extremely arduous and challenging undertaking for ourselves and even more challenging for the most adept of leaders. Cynicism within our population is firmly entrenched and is not likely to dissipate until real "people" leadership begins to emerge and Americans begin to trust in the future again.

We have also seen the demise of our faith in the family unit, traditionally viewed as a very strong self-corrective sociological mechanism and one seemingly capable of surmounting whatever sociological dysfunctions our society produced. Unfortunately, with more single households and an astronomical divorce rate the traditional family certainly cannot be expected to solve our social problems since we are not even sure what constitutes a functional family and how we might go about reestablishing it; this is especially true for particularly handicapped segments of our society. Given the extreme complexity of contemporary living, the ability to construct a truly functional family for the majority of our population is extremely dubious, especially as economic struggle becomes the dominant family characteristic and people have even less time available to focus on family needs.

Already, people are suspicious that maybe the traditional family is becoming somewhat of an anachronism; the divorce rate, the level of child abuse, and the general ineffectiveness of the courtship process all contribute toward the growing concern regarding the precariousness of the family and its future potential as a self-corrective sociological device. Our attempts to restore its once exalted position are done only half-heartedly, and although we may not want to admit it, we really doubt whether such attempts would do any good anyway.

Although this sentiment is largely unspoken, at least officially, most of us feel that it is nevertheless true. As proof, consider the political discussions regarding family values which are unquestionably less important relative to economic and defense issues in every successive campaign. It appears that we are beginning to reconcile the family's fate and we are not as concerned as we used to be with saving it in its traditional form.

The lack of a self-corrective mechanism is at the core of our sociological disillusionment. We simply do not have the same faith in our society that we used to have, and we need to construct a new faith if we are to heal. It is critical to remember, however, that this faith must necessarily be of a new kind and that the old faith, which today borders on naivete, is not only obsolete but undesirable. In order to establish a new faith, however, all of us must first be able to accept our individual responsibility to effectuate necessary change since only through our initiative and action can this change be possible; a reluctance to take initiative has become virtually ingrained in our psyches so we must not underestimate the degree of difficulty regarding this task. Prompt action is a high priority since the world is progressing at an extremely accelerated rate, taking us along in the fury of its progress, and as a result our solutions must come quickly, but without sacrificing effectiveness.

The "Threat" of Globalism

The development of a national self-corrective mechanism is further impeded by globalism. America has long been viewed, especially by us, as the world's last great hope, where liberty and the pursuit of happiness could be sought and attained; in short, America was where dreams could come true. Our culture's exaltation of the individual and our relative limitation of government involvement in individual lives produced a freedom and prosperity that came to be almost distinctly American, while the rest of the world was perceived by many of us as the great "encroacher" threatening our experiment with gradual, but destructive pollution. Our history has in a large part been the story of our attempt at forming a type of national and ideological purity as we fought foreign influences from nazism to communism while simultaneously ensuring that peoples from the globe could come to our country and put on the coat of Americana. In this endeavor, we felt purposeful and powerful.

Our national pride, to the point of ethnocentrism, was our self-corrective mechanism, the faith in our ideals and our principles the guiding hand of our national purpose and identity. Somehow, even though we were a racial and cultural melting pot, we formed a collective consciousness that for the most part transcended the ever present ingredients for strife and disintegration that such a mixture naturally contains. This "accommodation" of divergence was at the forefront of our national worth. But now, through the phenomenon of globalism, we are beginning to lose that. We are increasingly influenced by a world that does not possess our distinctly individual heritage or our experience with the accommodation of divergence so characteristic of our nation's past and so singularly responsible for our success. Is it a coincidence that as we have become involved to a much greater extent in the world's affairs that the size of our government has grown to such unthinkable levels, itself an anathema to our founding principles, and that we appear to have lost the collective consciousness of what it means to be an American? Is it surprising that as we become more involved in attempting to solve the world's problems without first solving our own, that we invite such ridicule and castigation from much of the world community?

Although this is not to suggest that we are being "tainted" by contemporary Medeas or that this line of logic is a plea for a return to some sort of economic and cultural protectionism, it is an exhortation that our ideological leadership is being threatened because we are diffusing the very collective sense of what it means to be American. The beauty of America has always been the generally accommodative and yet formative nature of our socio-political system. We can never make the assumption that foreign democracies have or will have the same mission and intention toward the cause of the individual as we do or that their conception of liberty is as "pure" as our own. We have conducted the experiment longer than anyone else and we have had the responsibility for democratic innovation as well as preservation. This is why our failings are both so glaring and so tragic; they have always carried the hopes of most of humanity with them, and it is also why we must develop a new strategy for maintaining our leadership in the arena of personal liberty and personal responsibility.

As a result, I am not advocating a return to the past but rather an advance into the future. We cannot allow a dysfunctional globalism to shape the world's future as it most assuredly will do if its present form is not altered. As the geopolitical battle ground moves away from military to economic competition, ideological leadership will shift to those countries with the strongest economies, not necessarily to those with the greatest vision for humanity. Foremost for us, we must understand that if we are to maintain our ideological leadership we must first win the economic competition and improve upon our own concept of freedom and upon our concept of individualism. We must understand that we have contributed to the bastardization of individuality, the global "taint" on what it means to be free, and that our past has cost us much credibility. We must now provide the emerging force of globalism with an injection of new thought on what constitutes freedom and how absolutely vital is the link between freedom and a higher quality of life. We have not been perfect, but we can learn from our mistakes and impart to the rest of the world the knowledge gained through a two-hundred-plus year struggle for freedom and individual responsibility.

The Power of People

The problems confronting the world are enormous, although well within the scope of what humanity, in a concerted effort and hopefully with the experience of American leadership, can accomplish. There can be no question that we as a species have created virtually incomprehensible triumphs over nature through our ability to think and reason, and that we have come to understand much about ourselves and our place within the universe. America, through the vision of our forefathers and our historical commitment toward an ever-evolving individualism, has led the expedition that extends the humanly possible; only recently have we begun to capitulate our leadership role through the decline of our culture.

Most of what needs to be accomplished is attainable if we will only assert ourselves toward a leadership function designed to be much more inclusionary than in the past. If the American people, with full commitment and fresh insight, will take it upon themselves to lead the journey into the human potential, all of humanity will benefit. Is there a greater leadership than this? Could we actually do more to further our own position than leading the world, through our example, toward new heights in which all of humanity benefits?

Nothing is more of an obstacle in this challenge than irresolution, so we must first strive for vision and diligence. We must believe in people and in their ability to improve their situation through an advancement of their reason and of their knowledge. We must know that information leads to knowledge and knowledge to power, and we must also know that the facilitator of this transition is choice and personal responsibility. We must believe that people, actual individuals, not only make a difference, but are the most powerful means at our collective disposal.

One of the prime obstacles to achieving our success in this pursuit of individual power is the alienation of people, what amounts essentially to a type of powerlessness and loss of hope from the very individuals most vital to the endeavor. We simply cannot accomplish what needs to be accomplished without the efforts of people, for it is people who have caused whatever successes we have achieved. If we do not get people involved, we cannot win. If we do not get people to put their faith in themselves, we have no hope.

In many ways, then, this book is about how to eliminate alienation so individuals can control their own destinies and determine their own futures. Mostly, it is about how to believe in yourself by first understanding what has collectively failed in the system and then how to utilize individually driven corrective measures that ultimately allow for the development of a more positive and purposeful existence. This book is therefore about the requirement for an individual openness to change and an individual amenability toward real self-evaluation; it is not about retribution, but rather about intensity and commitment for knowing oneself; it is also thus not about blame, but rather about promise.

It is my position that we can no longer rely on institutions or someone else to ensure our futures; we must do so ourselves. Almost all of the great movements throughout history are really stories of ideas gradually embraced by the masses, who, through their actions, cause collective change to happen. We have not witnessed great movements in this country for quite some time, and it would seem that we are due one. People are still the strongest known social force, as the recent events in the old Soviet sphere have again demonstrated. If we can develop a plan, a movement if you will, that promotes a new freedom designed to assist us in these increasingly complex and uncertain times, then we can ensure that the human family is prepared for the future. Why is this true? Because freedom is the prerequisite, the framework, which makes the fulfillment of the human potential at least possible. Without freedom and a reliance on the individual, we will ultimately fail. Without each individual's commitment toward individualism, we will lose.

The New Individualism

The idea behind the movement which we so desperately need is what we can term the "new individualism." This is not a call for the individualism of Locke or a form of narcissism, but rather an individual responsibility toward change of the individual that leads to a vastly improved and correctly formed collective whose primary characteristic is the universally held belief in the power of individuals for self-determination in all matters once the illusions and ignorance inherent in the system are significantly reduced. This belief does not seek to limit the role of government in the Lockean tradition, but instead promotes a collective consciousness that may be government at its finest; the government of the future could well be one in which there is greater government involvement in the instillment of real individualism in order to guarantee more individual liberty. Government may actively seek to promote individualism as a policy, legislating individual responsibility as law, as opposed to the current practice of constraining government in some deference to market forces or "invisible hands."

Conventional wisdom in this country, what is really conservative wisdom, has postulated that less government meant more individual responsibility since people are inherently responsible. Time has shown that many people, without demonstration, are not. Liberals, on the other hand, have historically tried to use government as a vehicle for controlling humanity's "darker" side until humanity became perfect. Both have been wrong in their philosophies since the real goal of government is to promote individual responsibility and choice through policies that ensure that people make their own, fully informed choices. Both conservatives and liberals have attempted to use government for their own self-interested purposes, and both have done so to the detriment of people since neither of their positions ensures that people make their own rational determinations. For conservatives, single individuals are somehow not as capable as market forces; for liberals, people are not yet capable. Both positions short-sell the human ability.

The new individualism is thus a fundamental trust in people and in their abilities, judgements, characters, and intellects. This movement goes beyond the concept of culture; what is required is a mental paradigm shift that transcends culture or sociological conditioning and that liberates all of us through the acceptance not only of our right toward self-determination, but also of our responsibility toward it. Furthermore, it is the recognition that people, indeed ourselves, are the only ones who can make the difference and transform the dysfunctional to the functional.

More than any other concept, the new individualism is about people. It is by definition anti-conformity since what is expected and required is for each individual to think and choose for himself/herself. The only thing absolutely certain in life is choice, but with choice comes individual responsibility; once this is understood it becomes evident that the only functional self-corrective mechanism is ourselves.

The advent of universal individual responsibility is not only historically possible, but rooted in evolutionary biology as well. The development of a truly functional self-corrective mechanism is Darwinian in that individually caused self-correction is our species' adaptive response to external pressures which are threatening our preservation. The inexorable forward march of history and biology is demanding that we adapt to new realities, specifically the ability to become, as a species, individually responsible for our actions and their effects on the larger whole. We must now accept that only through individual responsibility can we manage the collective and ensure that our species survives to reach its full potential.

The new individualism, like all adaptive responses, is at first largely unnoticed, gaining widespread recognition only when it affects a sufficiently large percentage of the population. We are quickly approaching that point when sociologically people are beginning to almost instinctually know that a dramatic change is necessary and forthcoming. Currently, this is being culturally expressed as a general feeling of frustration, a slippage of control, and a need for some form of change or remedial action. These are the first inklings that an adaptive response is indeed taking shape; it may have already taken a form, and soon it will proliferate. This is an extremely promising state of affairs since without this stage we could not progress to meliorative courses of action.

Invariably, the forces of conservatism and ignorance will fight to oppose the adaptive response and through their actions seek to ensure that it does not succeed in positioning humanity for a more promising future. This knee-jerk reaction proves that the evolutionary progression of human reason has a long way to go; the single biggest miscalculation these opponents will make is that we are somehow distinct from the history of the universe and not simply another species inhabiting the planet. They must see that evolution affects us as much as any other animal and they must also understand that their reluctance to change increases the likelihood of their own extinction.

The forces arrayed against the adaptive response are most threatening in one simple way: their fear and ignorance may not only guarantee their own demise, but ours as well. Most of us would like to believe that they will fail because the human drive to survive is greater than the human fear of failure. A large part of this survival drive is the need to control what we create and for what purpose, and in the future we will increasingly ask how this can be more readily and benevolently accomplished. This question is the driving force behind the new individualism, and hopefully we are asking it in time.

The New Individualism and Technology

The individual responsibility advocated here, what we can call the new individualism, must include the control and exploitation of technology for the liberation of the human spirit. In the future, technology must focus on the furtherance of human freedom and advance the full complement of the human potential. As part of our responsibility, we must exercise technological options that can be managed and that in no way harm the source of our sustenance, Earth.

The movement to control technology and thus protect the environment is itself an evolutionary phenomenon, an adaptive response designed for preservation of our home and of ourselves so that we might continue to live. It will also be our responsibility to live well. The control of technology that promotes a preservation of the planet and a higher quality of life facilitates a general feeling of "living well" and ensures that subsequent generations will also have the same opportunities as we do to prosper and control their own destinies.

If we can framework technological development to meet rational human ends, then we no longer need to fear technology since we will be directing its course and determining its objectives. Technology is nothing more than a testament to the powers of the human mind, and if we are ultimately responsible for technology, any failures within technological progression are our own inherent deficiencies; we simply cannot disassociate technology and our responsibility to manage it. Technology cannot be feared when we rationally control our creation.

Lastly, technology is an extension of the human will. Fundamentally, it is an effort for humankind to extend our reach beyond our grasp and within this context technology is not fearful, but hopeful. The pursuit of technology is nothing more than a "what if" question and is therefore akin to that part of the human spirit which seeks a better tomorrow through the vision of how today can be improved. The relationship between individual responsibility and the management of technology, indeed the creation of a better tomorrow, is intrinsic. And the purpose of this book is to demonstrate how to assume that responsibility and construct for ourselves the framework whereby we can achieve that future.

2
Fear

If we are to create for ourselves a better tomorrow through an increased self-responsibility and a new individualism, then we must first understand what we are up against. Most conventional analyses would probably focus on a relatively narrow band of what is perceived to be possible within an accepted "thinking" or within a "normal" range of choices, and would thus fail to properly identify the culprit; this is analogous to "fine-tuning" some instrument whose applicability is assumed. But what if the instrument is wrong? What if to be successful in our endeavor required a new instrument, a new way of measuring and looking at something?

Too often, the approaches we utilize fail to see the root causes of problems because they focus almost exclusively on refining what exists; since what exists is almost invariably something added to an existing base, the base is rarely questioned. If we are to proceed with a new individualism, we must examine the "bases" on which the past has been constructed and we must look at our base nature, the physical, biological, and cultural parts of ourselves which cause us to be who we are.

When we examine the incongruent nature of the "system" in which we live, we must proceed to the most base to find solutions. If we have failed to previously ascertain answers, then this says much about the process we use and about ourselves. What we might really be saying is that there is some limiting factor, inherent in us, that keeps us from progressing even though we have often dreamt about how the world might be different.

We have clearly demonstrated a lack of confidence and a distrust in our abilities; in short, we have been afraid that we will not be successful in the pursuit of an improved us. We are fundamentally most fearful of our inadequacy and so the most "base" is therefore fear.

To proceed with the new individualism, we must examine the concept of fear, for this is our most limiting factor. This examination, however, will discuss only the basic nature of fear and how it relates to the overall framework of this book; certainly, a comprehensive examination of fear would be beyond what is necessary for this discussion. It is also worth noting, however, that because of the extreme relevance and importance of the concept of fear, as well as its inexorably limiting effects on the human potential, the relatively brief discussion here should never be considered a substitute for a further in-depth analysis. If we, as a society, more closely examined the subject of fear such a study would greatly improve the chances of success in all that we do.

Fear as a Constraint on the Human Potential

Fear is sinister in its machinations and dire in its consequences. There is probably no other component within the human form so harmful to the human spirit nor none so pervasive. But fear is biologically rooted in our species, and is therefore fundamental to our existence. Fear feels natural, and we know that being fearful has occasionally worked to our advantage. Anything natural feels like it should be maintained, even promoted, and so we are reluctant to part with it since it feels like a part of ourselves.

In other words, we are aware that fear is a natural part of being and so developing strategies that significantly reduce or eliminate fear are usually undertaken only half-heartedly because we are not really convinced that we ought to. Unfortunately, the fear necessary for biological survival can act as a constraint on the human potential; though we would like to believe otherwise, there are still large parts of the human brain which, according to the Papez-MacLean theory of brain evolution, are more reptilian or mammalian than human and are thus more instinctual than rational; in short, a large percentage of our brain reacts from primal fear and not from logic. This is significant because it explains why so often we cannot rationally eliminate unwarranted fears or limiting thought patterns, and this also explains why our "fight or flight" reaction occurs so strongly in situations which offer no reasonable justification for it.

We tend to react fearfully at first to most stimuli, at least until we gain a familiarity or comfortability with them, and as a result we sacrifice time and opportunities because we are unnecessarily cautious or afraid. The result is often a form of conservatism which dominates our life and precludes us from considering alternatives which might potentially improve the quality of our living experience. Fear, then, produces a general hesitancy in our being that transcends what is biologically necessary for our survival and often precludes ventures into new, growth areas.

Our general level of awareness regarding the limiting nature of fear is very low. Part of this results from the natural presence of fear and some occurs because our social system is not designed to reduce or eliminate it. There are even those who would argue that some elements within the system, presumably power elites, intentionally allow the system to perpetuate this deficiency for their own selfish purposes. This last point appears highly conspiratorial, but there is nevertheless some probable truth to the fact that certain power elites in all countries fail to promote liberation policies that reduce fear because such policies are viewed as threatening to the existing power structure.

Although controversial, there is certainly the possibility that there are those who prefer that the majority of humankind never fully comprehend how fear has constrained the human potential, nor would they want the average citizen to realize the benefits from such an understanding. After all, even our most benevolent of leaders have their own biological predispositions, of which fear is certainly one. Within such a formulation, then, society can be seen not only as a composition of fearful members, but also as a collection of people sometimes victimized by a leadership that promotes that fear due to its own fear of ouster and loss of power.

In addition, the system fails through faulty design to eliminate fear among its members. After all, if individuals barely recognize the existence of fear, much less the role it plays in their lives, doesn't it seem likely that the collective continuation of fear occurs because of a dysfunctional, even ignorant system? We must remember that historically we are not that far removed from the time when we lacked the ability to reason and that the progression of reason is proceeding at a natural evolutionary rate; previously, then, we lacked the mental wherewithal to include a reduction of fear within our system.

What is most important to remember, however, is that through some biological and cultural deficiency we have not produced a vehicle sufficiently capable of reducing fear, and that we as a species have suffered unnecessarily because of it. As a remedial recourse, we must look at the sociological conditioning process as it relates to fear, understand it, and then develop strategies to correct the problem. We must contemplate what the reduction of fear would mean for our lives, embrace that vision, and work to make that vision a reality. But to develop that vehicle, we must look even further into the base of fear.

The Origin of Fear

What is the origin of fear? We have already identified the biological foundation for fear, but we also need to examine how the socialization process contributes to our fear-basing. As almost everyone knows, a large part of our socialization results from our relationship with our parents and our perception of what that relationship means for us. If we accept the premise that this relationship is critical and enduring in the formulation of who we perceive ourselves to be, then as a corollary any fears contained within would generally continue over time. These fears would be more or less rooted, the prevailing dynamic of the relationship becoming the standard for all relationships. If we see society as a system of relationships, this prototype becomes significant indeed since all relationships will assume some of the characteristics of our relationship with our parents.

Now, let's assume the prevailing dynamic is one of superior/inferior where the parents are in the superior position and the child in the inferior. The reality of the relationship is that the child needs the parents for his/her survival. At some point, the child realizes that he/she is dependent upon the parents and that the parents are in the "power" position; to some extent, then, the parents control the child and the child is more or less powerless, at least in certain circumstances. Clearly, even within this initial relationship, there is a power dynamic in which power or control become a worthy goal. The lack of power can easily become a fear of not having power.

We have all been children. We have all felt the feeling of powerlessness, of not being in control, and of being subject to the wishes of others. There is fear associated with a lack of power since we all want our way and to not have it is indeed quite fearful. The fact that when we are children our very lives depend on others, causes, at some level, a fear that we are somehow inadequate since if we were truly capable, we would have unlimited power; this awareness of our relative powerlessness is insecurity and it stays with us until we decide that we are sufficiently capable.

Now let's proceed to the system level. What does it mean for the system if the majority of its members doubt their capabilities? What does it imply for a nation when a huge percentage of its people live with a fear, rooted in childhood and continuing at least until that childhood reality is understood, that all social interactions are relationships that must contain some superior/inferior dynamic? Isn't superior/inferior simply a form of zero/sum? Is it any wonder that society takes on the dysfunctional relationship characteristics of its people? Is it surprising that our organizations, corporations, institutions, and political parties seek the superior side of virtually every relationship? Doesn't it seem logical that given the socio/biological origin of fear we often fail to work together to solve problems and that we sacrifice opportunity by not cooperating? Is it a surprise that when we see someone else gain we often see it as our loss?

Natural Fear-Basing Gone Awry

Since a society is indeed comprised of individuals, we can assume that any underlying individual fears would extrapolate to the larger whole. If people are fearful and insecure regarding their abilities, isn't it rather obvious that the society would exhibit these same characteristics? Wouldn't a society of fearful individuals also be a fearful society? Wouldn't such a society dread whatever dependencies it possessed and avoid the suggestion of its own demise?

A significant part of America and American leadership lives in fear; this segment hates our dependencies and avoids discussion of our national deterioration. People who call this out, like author Paul Kennedy in *The Rise and Fall of the Great Powers*, are ridiculed by this segment and labeled alarmist or paranoid. But these critics are afraid to face their fears, afraid to contemplate what must be changed. Fear breeds conservatism because fear hates to leave what is known. To a large extent, then, much of our country is afraid to go forward, afraid to transform into something different. But there is nothing scary about moving forward as long as you are anchored in your own confidence and controlling your own future.

Let's consider an example. There has been much written and discussed regarding the North American Free Trade Agreement (NAFTA) which recently passed through Congress. But if we look at the opponents of NAFTA, if we look at their motivations, we can see that their response was rooted in fear: the fear of losing jobs, the fear of changing the status quo, the fear that the agreement might be environmentally disadvantageous, and the fear that NAFTA is an acceleration of a globalism that we are certain to lose. All of these fears could be mitigated, however, if the opponents of NAFTA believed that all parties would benefit from such an accord, including America, because America has as much to gain as anyone else and is as capable as any other country. The reluctance to embrace NAFTA comes from self-doubt, the belief that America won't measure up or that it cannot compete. The opponents of NAFTA certainly had some valid arguments against an accord, concerning guarantees and other "level playing field" issues, but these can and/or have been worked out. What was never really admitted by the opposition is the fear that says America is not its old, competitive self and that the agreement will hasten our economic deterioration because we have ourselves deteriorated.

To enhance our understanding of how deep-seated the fear dynamic really is and to understand why opposition like that to NAFTA occurs, let us consider a framework which, I'm convinced, is largely behind our cultural inability toward self-correction. There is always a debate between which frameworks in a society really impact people and which do not, but there are unquestionably some frameworks which have almost universal validity, even though they may be latent and thus largely unnoticed. One such framework has been especially harmful, for it has affected virtually all of our social institutions, from corporate culture to family to government. The framework is best illustrated by an example and a diagram.

I first heard of this example through a management consultant, Mike McCaffrey, who had been influenced by William Glasser who wrote *Reality Therapy* and other fine works. As he said, the experience has the potential to change lives and certainly this can be true.

Let's assume that a woman is talking on the phone with someone and she realizes that she must be across town in fifteen minutes, although the trip from her office to the destination takes thirty minutes. Obviously, she is going to be late. She tells the person with whom she is talking to that she "must go" and "cannot talk anymore." The other party on the phone asks for just one more minute, but she tells the person that "I have to go, I have no choice" and she hangs up the phone and begins her journey across town.

Well, she has to go, right? Not exactly. She could call and cancel, she could send a substitute, she could reschedule, or she could just simply not go and face the consequences. The point is that she has choices, actually far more than I have listed here. She is, however, operating under the mental model that she in fact has no choice and so she reasons she must get across town as soon as possible. Her mental model limits her options, and by operating under such a worldview, she is denying herself the chance to create more favorable alternatives that could significantly improve her situation.

People make choices everyday. If we are alive, we must make choices, even if the choice is just to stay alive. Living means making choices, and so each individual has the responsibility to make their own choices and to choose on a daily basis. As a result, when we box ourselves in with the belief that we have no choices, that we are forever optionless and at the mercy of some larger and directing external force, we deny our natural right to choose. If we choose to live, we must make choices.

When humanity lives with the mental model that we have no choices, we live in an illusory state. All we have is choice. Most importantly, to limit our choices, to believe that we do not have any options, is to live in fear; when we live in fear because of a false perception that the future offers no real choices, we can become desperately dependent on what exists today, and that is no way to live.

The above example is best illustrated by the following diagram:

"I cannot"	"I can"
"I have to"	"I want to"

▲
CHOICE

Humanity has lived its existence largely to the left of the CHOICE point, which, in fact, is an illusion and therefore does not exist. If we now combine what we know about natural socio-biological fear with the above diagram, it is easy to see how society has evolved from a base human fear, i.e. that there are forces beyond our control, to a grouping of people and their institutions that perpetuate the belief that you have no choices and thus life must be a fearful proposition. Almost all of our sociological conditioning process reinforces the belief that we have no choice, that life dictates to us, and that we are at the mercy of forces that control us. If we have no options, something else or someone else must be in control.

The reality of life is far different. We have choices. Fear may be a natural part of life, but it does not need to limit or control us. The new individualism, then, embraces everything to the right of the CHOICE point, for that is what is real. Within that embrace lies the hope of our species, for only in every individual choice can come the personal resolve that makes us whole.

The Effect of Death

The greatest tragedy of all is the wasting of life and the incredible opportunities that living presents because we falsely perceive that we have no choices. When we think of the way that people often live their lives, afraid to consider alternatives because they violate or oppose existing beliefs, then we can begin to understand the tragedy of how fear limits the human potential, not only for accomplishment, but for happiness as well. Now let's examine the extreme of this fear and use the subject of death to further demonstrate this point and to show the interrelationship between our fear of death and the belief that we have no choices.

Think of the many people who never examine the possibilities of life due to an excessive fear of death. In this way, it becomes evident that a "no-choice" mental model positions death as a further confirmation that someone else is in control of our lives, that death is more than some final biological act, and that the inevitability of death is in fact a continuing, daily affirmation of a life lived without real choices.

The point here is simple: death to many people is the event that validates all of the sociological conditioning process emphasizing personal powerlessness. For them, the recognition that death is inevitable substantiates the belief that people have no choices and no power, and ultimately do not control their own lives. How tragic indeed to contemplate the sum of lost human opportunity simply because of this belief.

Given the above, it thus seems logical to assume that fear came first and that we created our entire social structure around fear. A clue might be what we first sought to create. It has been said that the organizing principle behind every society is for war. And what is war? It is, in part, the desire to be strong to protect yourself against those that you perceive would destroy you or cause you harm. War is therefore fundamentally rooted in a fear that resides in the self-preservation instinct itself, and so the organizing principle behind every society is thus not really for war, but rather for the elimination of fear in order to feel secure. And the fundamental fear embedded in the self-preservation instinct is the fear of death.

The net effect of death has been a limitation of the human potential through a denial of possibilities; our entire social structure reaffirms our perception that we have no choices and that we are ultimately under the control of forces greater than ourselves. When we fail to understand what the possibilities of life can be, we resign ourselves instead to a continuation of a life lived with an illusory, unjustified fear. Moreover, fear, like all cancers, spreads to other parts of our being, further debilitating us through the devastation inflicted on related elements within our composition; let's look at some of these now.

Pain Avoidance

Although the lack of an examination of death is probably the most dramatic example of how, through our fear, we fail to maximize the living experience, there are certainly other lesser fears that cause us to forsake much opportunity in living. One of these is the fear of pain. The desire to avoid pain is a very strong human drive, both from a physical and an emotional standpoint, and it is oftentimes amazing at the lengths in which people will go to avoid pain.

What many people fail to understand is the advantageous positioning that successful negotiation through painful territory can mean for their lives. We are biologically and culturally predisposed to avoid pain, and as a result, we develop ways to ensure that we limit the number of painful experiences; unfortunately, this can also preclude us from experiencing the process of pain, which, although certainly not pleasant, can lead to growth and understanding and ultimately toward more meaningful and fulfilling ways to live.

Interestingly, our preconditioning toward lack of choice often precludes us from experiencing the benefits of negotiation through pain. Since we largely see ourselves possessing no real choices, we believe that we don't have any choice other than to avoid pain. We fail to see that we can choose to gain through pain and that there is much to be derived from the understanding that results after we move beyond it.

If we can begin to accept that pain is a temporary state that can lead to much potential benefit, then we have less to fear and less need to control. This is the key point: when we successfully fight through pain toward a new understanding, we also reduce the amount of fear in our lives and construct for ourselves a growing confidence to handle similar situations in the future.

Naturally, the first opportunities to fight through pain will be the most challenging and thus it is logical to expect a high failure rate. Eventually, however, there will be successes and increasingly we would almost welcome painful situations as opportunities to better understand ourselves and to improve the quality of life. Any corrective measure that either individuals or societies utilize in the drive to improve themselves must include some "pain management" and a commitment to use pain for a constructive purpose. The new individualism, then, must necessarily use pain to grow beyond current boundaries and must promote courage, opportunity, and vision to overcome the innate human desire to avoid pain.

Anxiety

When we fail to negotiate through pain, however, we develop increasingly sophisticated methods of pain avoidance, even though we know that painful experiences are unavoidable. The dread, even fear, of future pain is anxiety. We truly fear painful situations, which are replete in our individual and collective consciousnesses, and so we try to avoid similar situations in the future. We not only do this personally, but culturally as well.

A quick example. The Vietnam war experience demonstrates how we have tried to avoid pain as a culture through our avoidance of equivalent wars simply because Vietnam was indeed very painful; this, in part, helps to explain the reluctance to undertake extended military operations like that in Somalia since they might turn into other Vietnams and become painful situations.

The pervasiveness of anxiety is well-documented, both in individuals and in societies. America is especially burdened with enormous levels of anxiety, exacting a heavy human toll in the form of much physical and emotional strain, because our system demands so much from its people. Moreover, our social system does little if anything to provide anxiety relief; the current state of the economy, with low growth rates, corporate restructurings, and increasingly large knowledge requirements is a great example of how over time we tend to increase the anxiety burden without developing effective ways of managing, both on an individual and a national level, the stresses such a system produces.

But why is anxiety so pervasive and so harmful? Why does it appear that we are so ill-equipped to handle anxiety? What is it that causes us to accelerate toward an anxiety spiral that offers little hope of restraint?

Standard wisdom cites contemporary living as the primary source of anxiety, what with traffic congestion, pollution, career competition, child-rearing, the business cycle, information overload, drug and alcohol abuse, global economic competition, and a million other social stresses fraying the social fabric; however, this explanation is oversimplistic and lacking, as usual, a more base explanation.

What our society is really missing is the lack of time available for introspection, both personal and national; this shortage of time precludes us from knowing who we are and what we want and hinders us from developing strategies that might more effectively manage anxiety. The point here is simple: if we make more time available for knowing ourselves, we can significantly reduce anxiety by eliminating things that are unimportant in the overall scope of living, many of which are extremely stressful and dispose us toward further anxiety. There is not time to do everything, only time to do what we want and what fulfills us. If we really believe in ourselves, we can even structure our careers and the economic necessities of life around what we need to be personally fulfilled. If we trust in our capabilities, this can really happen.

The belief in the capabilities of the self extends to the sociological level as well. Much of societal anxiety could be managed with a collective vision. If we will tackle our problems directly, seeking more options and possibilities for success, we could transform society in a relatively limited amount of time. If we are serious about wanting to eliminate anxiety, we must promote in all of us a sense of perspective on what we think is truly important and what we believe will make us happy.

The path to collective improvement runs right through the individual. We cannot collectively control anxiety until we individually decide to do so. And wishing it were different or nostalgically remembering less complicated days will do nothing to remedy our problems since only individual effort, purposeful and focused, has any chance of providing a more promising future. We must accept that our passivity has done much to create the current sociological condition, where a state of anxiety and some sense of hopelessness exists, and then find ways, again individually, to reduce or even eliminate our quiescence.

Expectations

If the base reason behind much of our anxiety is fear, and we know that much of fear is illogical, then many of the assumptions supporting our anxiety must also be illogical. In short, the premises behind our fears and anxieties often lack rational justification. If many of our "support" premises are indeed illogical, then much of what we experience will be disappointing because our expectations have little chance of being realistically fulfilled.

A good example of this might be our assumption that love is magical and requires no maintenance or work to endure. We expect that once we fall in love it will last and that the beauty of the initial romance will continue unabated and even intensify. Reality may be much different; a good loving relationship requires tremendous amounts of work, patience, and understanding, which, especially for our young people, is never adequately discussed in the prevailing cultural ethos.

But what is behind the "failure" of our expectations framework? What are we really doing when we expect?

There is another, much more base, aspect of expectations which is incredibly revealing: expectations are actually a form of control designed to reduce fear. All of us prefer a known quantity because the unknown scares us; as a result, in almost any situation we produce some expectations designed to ensure that we maintain some form of control, although as people, many of life's experiences are beyond our ability to adequately prepare for them. But because of our fear, we avoid these experiences whenever possible. As a result, we preclude, through an inflexibility that allows us to participate in only those things that we can control, many of life's possibilities. Within this framework, then, expectations can be seen as our attempts to control life itself and they are an actual mechanism that we have developed in order to feel more secure in a world which we oftentimes perceive as extremely precarious.

Given the above logic, it is not much of a stretch to understand how some people might become bored with living since virtually all of the potential surprises are removed in a life dominated by control. Clearly, then, there is a link between fear, anxiety, expectations, and a boring life. Boredom can be fundamentally the fear associated with trying new things. The key to living exciting lives, then, is to overcome our fears of considering alternatives and expose ourselves to new experiences because we welcome the opportunity that such adventurism brings.

When we seek to live in control, we exist in a state contrary to nature itself, for nature is fundamentally random, and to live with a rigid mindset is thus disharmonious with the flow of life. Our efforts at control work against our own purposes, for such efforts are actually extremely insidious manifestations of our own misguided and illusory attempts to gain a perceived security that tragically exists, more often than not, only in illusion. If we can find the confidence to embrace the natural order, we can enjoy the opportunity afforded through the linkage between fundamental randomness and diversity.

As always, much of what applies for the individual can be extrapolated to the societal level. As a nation, we often expect things that have little chance of being realistically fulfilled because the foundational logic on which many of these expectations are based is flawed, and so many times we are disappointed in our results.

One such example is the false assumption made by our top political leaders that other nations logically desire to be just like us; obviously, this was much more true a generation or two ago, but our imperial attitude to this day still infuriates many in the world community. Our ethnocentric belief in our way of life has been a very costly national lesson indeed: Vietnam and to some extent the Middle East are but two examples of places where our ethnocentrism has been flatly rejected. What we have had to learn is that although other nations may opt for a democratic/capitalistic form of political/economic arrangement, their construct of it must still be their own.

The new individualism has a big role to play in the "re-creation" of expectations; the hope that it offers concerns the self-responsibility of both people and nations to develop realistic, achievable goals. In the future, expectations will change from a vehicle of control to a device that assists in the construction of the humanly possible.

Alienation

As we reduce fear through the recognition of our control/expectation techniques and open ourselves up to the creation of options, we will make tremendous gains in minimizing another of the liabilities of a fear-based existence: individual and collective alienation. To a large extent, this alienation has resulted from our relative inability to create alternatives and to develop realistic expectations. The ability to create options is an extremely important effort for us since, if successfully undertaken, it will propel us toward creating a more propitious framework for both personal and national goals.

Why have we been so alienated? What in our system has forced us into increasingly narrower paths? Let's start with our economic structure. There can be no question that contemporary economics forces people into increasing levels of specialization simply to remain competitive; there are, of course, costs involved in specialization. Moreover, everyone is affected by the economic system, and so if we have been "forced" to become more specialized it is only natural that we simultaneously lost touch with diversity. In many ways, we have become our jobs and our careers have become our vision of who we are.

The point here is simple: we have bought into specialization as a means of economic furtherance and necessity, but we have rarely questioned to what extent or degree our participation limits our individual self-awareness. We do not have a clear picture because we have failed to create options that might have shown us, if not exactly a different course, then at least a more balanced one.

Moreover, there has also been the underlying fear that a failure to specialize might somehow decrease the probability of success; only now, and after much alienation, have we begun to realize the benefits to be gained from the creation of options. Throughout the world people are beginning to question, and in some cases act against, the alienation produced by the system of specialization. The collapse of communism can, to some degree, be seen in this light since a command system offers little in individual or cultural diversity. A more relevant example is probably the lifestyle revolt in Japan that is actually a corrective movement aimed at achieving a more balanced and less alienated existence. The Japanese have farther to go than we do, but it makes for a good example of how the specialization process can alienate people from themselves and so adversely affect the system's participants that they must ultimately seek a new order in which to rediscover themselves.

To initiate a change of lifestyle away from imbalance and toward symmetry, either personally or culturally, is a bold, courageous step that must fundamentally address the base fear behind our unwitting contribution to the process of alienation. We must ask again why we are afraid to seek balance and why we are afraid to step out of our normal operational mode and try something new.

To overcome the fear of trying new things, we need to look at some examples of where and how we are succeeding in this endeavor. Perhaps the best work in this area is being done in the field of management.

There is presently a movement in this country to make our companies more globally competitive by unleashing the creative abilities of people within these organizations by liberating them from bureaucratic constraint and rigid mindsets. This is true for both managers and for employees. Companies have become much more horizontal and less hierarchical in an attempt to better serve the customer and liberate the employee who is closest to the client. Most importantly, this organizational change has produced the net effect of making the employee much more responsible for the work to be done and less alienated. As a result, the employee has developed a sense of ownership in the enterprise which, of course, produces tremendous benefits for the company. Although such management practices are still the exception, where they have been tried they are often producing fantastic results.

We need to develop, in addition to a business management theory, a people theory that is designed to provide a framework whereby people can more readily expose themselves to the benefits derived from self-responsibility. People who know themselves and what they want and need from their lives are less alienated and less directed by fear; in short, they are more confident and thus capable. Such an attitude will no doubt prove contagious and will spread to government and other social institutions. The new individualism promises to be exactly the kind of "people theory" that serves to mitigate in a very significant way the alienation that has come to almost characterize our current system. And if we implement such a theory, it will do much to eliminate the most destructive by-product of alienation: disinterest.

Disinterest

Alienation produces in people a severance from both themselves and their society, and the realization of this severance often causes the belief that singular efforts rarely matter or have little chance of effecting the larger whole; the resulting lack of effort or motivation is disinterest. When people feel alienated, out of touch with themselves and the human drive for social interaction and cause, they are also disinterested in the human condition. When we fail to be interested in humanity, we fail to be interested in who we are.

In many ways, it is advantageous to view disinterest as a by-product of alienation for in this way we can see how the former results from the latter and how left unchecked contributes toward a gradual deterioration of both people and country. Disinterest is especially threatening to the well-being of a nation, for without the interest of people in national affairs, democratic governments inevitably collapse.

It stands to reason, then, that as alienation is reduced, so is the level of disinterest in our society; people, feeling that their lives and opinions matter, become increasingly involved in economic, political, and social concerns. The sociological benefit is, of course, tremendous since motivated citizens tend to produce a more participatory democracy, which, after all, is not only a purported national goal, but makes us more globally competitive as well. A participatory democracy, at least in theory, reduces corruption, waste, fraud, and fiscal mismanagement as people demand greater accountability within their governmental structure by virtue of their increased "ownership" in the system.

The current system operates in an almost diametrical fashion to the preferred outcome just discussed. Because of disinterest, we have let our concept of democracy get away from us and we must accept that our apathy is partly responsible for our angst. Our disaffection with our political and economic system is pervasive, and every subsequent failure seemingly proves that our system is incapable of self-correction; as these failures mount, we increase the collective level of disinterest.

Until we acknowledge our responsibility in correcting the problem, we cannot be successful in improving our society. The fight against disinterest is an honorable one, if for no other reason than that it greatly furthers the cause of the individual, in whom any collective benefit must begin. Disinterest directly suppresses the human will, and is therefore an enemy of people and nations that must be constantly fought. We must reduce disinterest so that we can be more interested, even passionate, about our work, our relationships, our social direction, and our country's future. If we can become more interested in ourselves, we can create a nation that is a mirror image of what we personally want to be.

The Reduction of Fear

Although we may never completely eliminate fear and its hazardous side effects, we can speculate what a substantial reduction of fear might mean for the course of human development and for our individual happiness; moreover, we can do this without being overly idealistic or naive. We can make this claim because there are people who actually do it, who really minimize their fears and live more complete and meaningful lives.

There is much promise in the reduction of fear. Foremost, a reduction of fear translates into increased opportunity through an exposure to diversity and the increased ability to recognize the benefits of process and randomness. Through this exposure, we will be more likely to risk, although not foolishly. Why? Because much of our behavioral history has been one of caution and restraint, resulting almost exclusively from our own fearful misperceptions and insecurity. If we can better trust our powers of reason and assume that rationality is the prerequisite for success, then we can also assume that due to our enhanced reasonableness we will better balance risk and opportunity.

The reduction of fear creates a healthier worldview through an increased reliance on reason and opportunity; it is not reasonable to live limited by fear. Humans have the unique ability to construct for themselves what they desire; such is the beauty of the power to reason. The liberation potential of a more rational worldview is extraordinary. If we can operate on the assumption that increased rationality is beneficial for both individuals and society, then the reduction of fear that serves to advance this reasonableness is not only crucial to the cause of human progression, but crucial to the construction of an environment in which that progression can flourish.

A reduction of fear thus creates a tremendous awareness of the human condition and makes us increasingly conscious of our relationship to the rest of the universe. As people begin to more fully understand and appreciate this relationship due to the "open-mindedness" that results from a diminishment of fear, there will be an increased sense of oneness and kinship toward both our species and our planet. This is certainly not a naive thought since there is ample historical precedent: whenever we have eradicated some disease or developed some advantageous technology, we have all felt a sense of pride in being human.

As a corollary to the above, our accomplishments and the control of our own futures destroys the reliance on teleology and instead ascribes individual responsibility and choice. When this occurs en masse, it will truly be a quantum leap for our species and will do more to ensure our survivability than any other thing we could possibly do.

The cost of failing to eliminate teleology is high. We can no longer afford to be at the mercy of "external" forces which ostensibly direct our lives. If we fail to move forward in our pursuit of the new individualism, then we will encourage fear's sinister by-products: personal and sociological disillusionment. Let's look at these next.

3

Disillusionment

We next need to examine what happens when we fail to move beyond a life dominated by fear. We need to see what happens when people fail to realize their dreams because of their own perceived inadequacies, and we also need to feel the sadness, the tragedy, of people who fail to look inward and instead cast blame on a system that is, in part, their own illusory creation. We need to understand the prison that the state of disillusionment invariably causes in people who fail to free themselves.

But disillusionment is not only an individual experience, it is a collective one as well. Societies, even the entire sum of the human family, can exist in a state of disillusionment, perplexed at how something as well-intentioned as our social creation can go so wrong. This must have been exactly the feeling when the Nazi concentration camps were first disclosed, as people no doubt wondered how humanity could stray so far from that side of us that longs for mutual understanding and respect. We must see that societies often become disillusioned because we have never formed a valid self-corrective mechanism, and so as a people we are subjected to recurring bouts of disillusionment that drain us of our focus and our purpose to do well.

What Is Disillusionment?

Disillusionment is really the incongruity between what people want and what their life experience has shown. In many respects, disillusionment is closely related to expectations and wants; often, an examination of disillusionment can reveal much regarding human needs and what people seek for themselves. People want quite a bit, at least initially, and we are frustrated and disillusioned when fear keeps us from moving to the point where we can fulfill our dreams.

Disillusionment is also the stage of life where illusion meets reality. Certainly, it can be one of the most trying periods in our lives and left unresolved it can greatly contribute toward alienation, isolation, powerlessness, hopelessness, trauma, and even death. I'm sure we all know someone who is disillusioned, and at one time or another, we have also been disillusioned ourselves and felt the anxiety associated with this mental state.

Without question, a protracted stage of disillusionment can be one of life's most tragic experiences as the loss of hope disillusionment causes invariably produces people who are less than their potential and who know it. Disillusionment devitalizes people and their cultures and inexorably threatens choice and self-responsibility. Disillusionment, then, imperils the new individualism in a very distinct way.

The Foundations of Disillusionment

If we can accept that our sociological conditioning reinforces our fear-based behavior and that much of these behaviors are unwarranted or unjustified, then maybe we can begin to develop a conditioning process that liberates instead of oppresses and which is, of course, more realistic and less illusory. The personal and social advantages that result from such an improved sociological conditioning process are legion and offer tremendous hope for the future.

Continuing with this logic, it would appear that much of our sociological experience has been a reaction against fear, and the form of this reaction was the creation of beliefs and values that, in many instances, were based on illusion. If the society is more likely to condition the individual than vice versa, then virtually everyone is at least partially a victim of such a dynamic. Herein lies the key to unlocking the individual: much of what we are is based on illusion, and as a result, much of what we have come to be is not real and exists, to a large extent, only in our minds.

Clearly, part of our personal and collective disillusionment results from the "false expectation framework" which our sociological conditioning process produces; in short, we expect things which do not occur in reality and the gap that exists between our expectations and what is possible causes disillusionment. Moreover, human beings are far more perceptive than we might otherwise believe and so this gap exists even before we consciously acknowledge it. Hence, we experience the incongruity and confusion which we have discussed earlier.

Often, there are accompanying feelings of anger and confusion since we know that we have often trusted in these illusions, even depended upon them, and the recognition of their falsehood can be quite devastating, leaving us ungrounded and searching for something to hold on to. We are often left with the feeling that something is missing and that life itself has deceived us, and we often feel that we can no longer trust others, our system, or ourselves.

As a result, disillusionment is often experienced as the destruction of confidence and the severing of yourself from yourself. Perhaps now we can see why this stage can be so traumatic; when the quintessential trust, the trust in oneself, is called into question, self-doubt begins in earnest. Disillusionment, then, can often preclude a longer-term perspective of hope, and unfortunately many people never realize that their ability to exit this stage lies in an honest evaluation of themselves and the society in which they live.

Sadly, many people simply cannot envision how to rebuild their base and start anew; if they could, they would take one of the first steps in dramatically improving their lives. The same is true for nations. We have built up so much, so many institutions and styles and characteristics, that it often seems inconceivable to start again or to even seriously reevaluate what works and what does not. We are afraid to reengineer our society the way some progressive companies are beginning to reengineer their organizations, and like those companies that stay in rigid, immutable structures, we have a strong likelihood of failure.

The Creation of Illusions

Before we can construct a method of overcoming disillusionment, we need to examine how illusions are created, why we rely on them, and why they are so difficult to eliminate. Without illusions, we could not become disillusioned. Everyone is saddled with illusions; our conditioning alone counts for innumerable ones, and it is completely natural to experience apprehension when we contemplate letting go of an illusion that has been with us for a long time and opt instead to seek the truth. But if we are to more fully develop ourselves and our cultures, we must undertake this challenge.

How do illusions get created? What is the process whereby we come to believe falsehoods? Almost invariably, they develop in childhood as a set of false thinkings, originating in that time of our lives when we lack the self-sufficiency and knowledge to formulate our own realistic perceptions; in short, we are unable to develop an accurate reality due to the illusory influence of "stronger" others, and because of this, these misconceptions become our own. Until this process is broken, these illusions are perpetuated from generation to generation. Some of these illusions are literally millenniums old, rooted in ignorance that even the forceful progression of history itself has yet to eradicate; this is a testament to their power.

Again, recall the initial relationship in our lives, that of parent/child. If the parent is living with illusory influence, then these same illusions usually become contagions caught by unsuspecting children. The Harlow study in psychology, which proved that we are in many respects exactly like our parents, is especially incriminating evidence that these illusions can be passed on to our children. A diagram may help to demonstrate the point here:

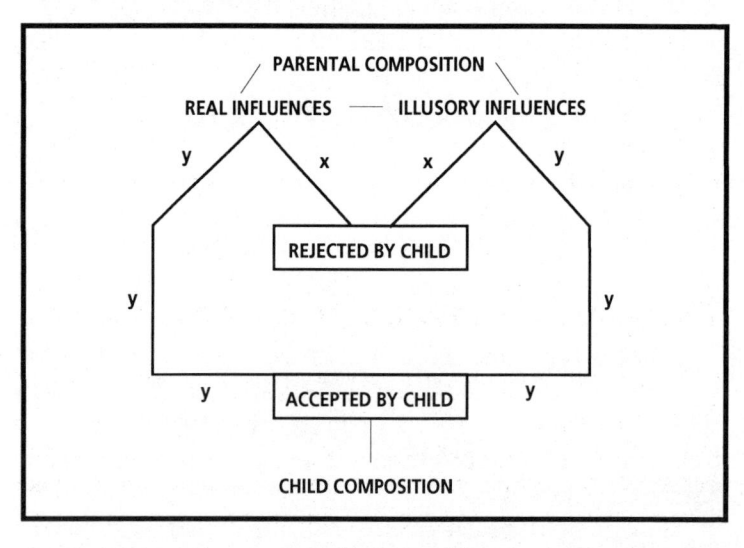

```
                    PARENTAL COMPOSITION
            REAL INFLUENCES  ——  ILLUSORY INFLUENCES
              y      x       x         y

                    REJECTED BY CHILD

         y                                      y


         y         ACCEPTED BY CHILD        y

                    CHILD COMPOSITION
```

As we can see, some of the real and illusory influences of the parents are rejected by the child, shown by the "x" lines, while some of the real and illusory influences of the parents are accepted by the child, shown by the "y" lines. The full composition of the child is thus formed by influences based on reality as well as on illusion. Obviously, the child would benefit most from a full acceptance of all real influences of the parents and would somehow find it within himself/herself, a highly unlikely prospect, to reject all illusory influences.

These early illusions are powerful conditioners that can last an entire lifetime unless people somehow find a way to really question their upbringing and the influence of their parents. If indeed our parental influence contains some illusory influences, we will certainly suffer if we do not find ways to eliminate them. Tragically, the cycle repeats itself until someone realizes the error and opts for an alternative. And, more often than not, the single greatest illusory influence perpetuated through the generations is the perception of individual inadequacy.

Now, if the perception of individual inadequacy is passed on to us through the parental dynamic, what does this say for a society comprised largely of parents? What does it mean for us since we are all once children? What does this say about the family? What does this say about a nation that is largely comprised of families and of a nation that promotes family in such a profound fashion?

The Dysfunctional Mental Model of the Collective

If the current family structure fosters illusory influences, then virtually all people are affected since almost everyone has been raised with some form of a family. Logically, it follows that whatever institutions develop from the family model would also take on some illusory influences. Never should it be assumed that we have eliminated illusory influences nor should we doubt that they have existed for a very long time.

To prove this latter point consider that history is replete with examples of illusory perceptions, passed from generation to generation, some of which seem to seriously question humankind's ability to act rationally; these include blood-letting, witch trials, and child-sacrifice to name only the more extreme examples. The point is that at any given time, society has illusory beliefs that not only guide its behavior and determine its policies, but form it's collective culture as well.

We have seen that social institutions have incredible conditioning powers on the individuals within that society, and that certainly it is a rare individual who understands the full extent of this conditioning process. Moreover, there can be little doubt that if the society conditions its people in an illusory manner, its citizens are thus greatly disadvantaged since succeeding in anything counts only if it is done within reality. Our reluctance to accept society's great influence on us, rooted in an insecurity that does not want to appear naive, actually hinders our emotional and spiritual development; if we are afraid to ask the questions, we cannot ascertain the answers.

We have also seen how it appears that ruling elites sometimes do not want individuals to engage in real self-pursuit since such activity can threaten their power. Ignorance is ruled more easily than intelligence. One of the best examples of this are certain televangelists who, even in a myriad of scandal, continue to receive contributions to swell their coffers and improve their standard of living while the contributors of theses funds are deluded into believing some form of altruism exists. To a large extent, these televangelists preserve their power through the perpetuation of an illusion, an illusion that attempts to demonstrate something which they are not.

People must begin to understand the relationship between the full extent of collective influences and the illusory nature of many of these influences if we are to reach our full potential. We must see society as a sometimes interwoven pattern of social illusions that contribute toward a collective disillusionment which stems from what we have been told and what our minds suspect or know. Moreover, we must understand how the full scope of illusory influences are assimilated by us if we are to have any hope of eliminating them; again, we must assume our responsibility toward their eradication and exercise our choice to shed their influence.

The Promise of Reason

Since illusions are rooted in ignorance and insecurity, we must use reason and confidence to eliminate them. Fortunately, the process of evolution works to our advantage; the progression of reason over time should position us to increasingly avail ourselves of illusions and therefore to comprehend reality more accurately.

To prove that rational evolutionary progression is occurring, think how far we have progressed in our understanding of something as simple as the familiar clap of thunder. In ancient times, humanity incorrectly surmised that the noise occurred due to a god or some other unexplained power and soon this rationale became the accepted explanation for thunder. We now know that there are physical reasons for thunder, a sound emitted after an electrical charge of lightning, and we now associate this noise with a physical understanding unknown to the first humans. Through reason, we have advanced our understanding of our world and shattered the illusion of thunder. This is an extremely simplistic example, but it nevertheless demonstrates the point that as humankind progresses further, using increased reason and knowledge, we will undoubtedly improve our understanding of reality.

Reason is the natural enemy of illusion. Reason creates options, and options provide more than one way of looking at something. Illusions are often no more than narrow-mindedness, a mental model saying that we have no choices and that someone or something else is in charge; moreover, reason knows that nothing is pre-determined and that we are ultimately in control of our own futures. Reason challenges precepts, our own as well as those of our society.

We can use our reason to liberate ourselves from illusory influences and to develop confidence which can greatly reduce the levels of fear in our lives; as reason opposes illusion, so does confidence oppose fear. With the tremendous expansion of reason today, we are clearly at an historically opportune time to reduce the amount of illusory influences in our lives, but only if we truly capitalize on this chance. We must tackle the full extent of our sociological conditioning and discard what we know to be illusory; only then, can we use the proliferation of knowledge to our advantage.

Reason does much to overcome the state of disillusionment; if we can use our minds, use our ability to reason, then we can do much to extricate ourselves from our disillusioned state and move forward toward new truth and understanding. Through our reason, we can change the sociological conditioning process to one that promotes the rationality of people and their choices. We can transcend the state of fear that left unresolved causes disillusionment, and we can begin to see how tomorrow can be improved.

Let's look at a few examples to prove the point: our political heritage, our religious background, and our economic system.

Our political heritage has contained many illusory, even hypocritical, influences. Some are incredibly fundamental, such as the gross disparity between a constitutional rhetoric that posited that "all men are created equal" and the existence, for much of our history, of slavery. Another fundamental example is the reliance on a completely capable individual, free to make his/her own choices because of an innate and aware human reasonableness, as posited by John Locke and Adam Smith. In reality, many people have failed to demonstrate this capability because they have lacked a good example of how to be self-responsible. More recently, Johnson's Great Society proved to be an illusory experience since it failed, in a dramatic way, to match the rhetoric of its stated objectives with what it actually accomplished and as a result Americans funded a pipe-dream. Look at an even more contemporary example. The 1980s was billed and promoted by the Reagan administration as a return to prosperity that would endure and virtually eliminate downturns in the business cycle. What we got were paper gains that almost bankrupted our country; this was a particularly tragic illusion that we are only now beginning to pay for.

What about religion? We have had enough religious hypocrisy to last a millennium. Moreover, think of the damage done to people because of a general religious philosophy that de-emphasizes the relative importance of this life compared to an afterlife. That this life counts only insofar as it contributes to something more lasting is an incredible illusion that deprives people the value of living. As we have seen, religion in general promotes ignorance and fear since it discourages explorative reason by threatening retribution for free-thinking. The opportunities to know yourself are virtually precluded if you adhere to this type of religious philosophy. If the mechanistic interpretation of the universe ultimately proves correct, where a "Big Bang" or some other scientifically explained phenomenon accounted for life as we know it, religion then will have been the greatest illusion of all.

The capitalistic system has never lived up to its billing. That it is the most preferred of all historically tried economic systems is not the same as total vindication for all its tenets. It has glaring weaknesses which are constantly downplayed by its proponents who forever invoke the comparisons to socialism; this comparison is a form of illusion. In reality, we actually have a mixed economy that contains many socialistic elements within it. This not only includes the traditional "common defense," but also includes education and infrastructure projects since these are socialist in that they are funded through redistribution of income for a common need. Moreover, look at much of current business theory; such concepts as small business units and self-directed work groups (which are essentially communal groups with a profit motive) combine socialistic and capitalistic features to produce more efficient and productive companies. The official, and we might add illusory rhetoric, fails to mention the socialistic nature of such practices.

Why are we afraid to tell the truth and admit that illusions exist? Why do we, through our shared culture, promote and encourage a misrepresentation of reality? Is it because we are fearful our children or ourselves will not be able to handle the truth? Are we afraid that the great experiment of our nation will come crashing down if we call out our shortcomings? Or are we secretly suspicious that we lack the courage and confidence to truly believe in ourselves? Are we afraid of the responsibility?

Breaking the Cycle of Illusion Perpetuation

We have talked about how history is presenting to us an opportunity to increase our comprehension of reality through the reduction of illusory influence. But exactly how do we break the cycle of illusion perpetuation and free ourselves from its limiting effects?

First, we must confront current reality and expose ourselves to a reality that questions the sum of our beliefs. Unfortunately, many people are almost thoroughly conditioned to avoid introspection so that they seldom question any beliefs, not only their own, but the prevailing cultural ones as well. This is why parenting is such a vital component within the context of broad sociological change, for proper parenting would provide greater numbers of introspective people who could cause constructive change on the system. If we can raise our children with a more rational outlook and a greater amenability toward change, then we can do much, simply through questioning, to circumvent illusory influences in our culture.

Second, we need to open up the educational process to the promotion of an individualism that is far more balanced than the current one; as a culture, we do a very poor job of cultivating for the individual anything outside of career or family responsibility, and it is rare to find people who understand that life can be much more than that. Our educational system, although in many respects generalist, does not cohere a well-rounded perspective for most people. The new individualism must address this system failure and instill in people the belief that knowing oneself and seeking balance are the keys to living more productive and happy lives. Although proper parenting and formal education certainly do much to reduce illusory influence within our culture, we need something to further this process as we move through life. Remember, the current social structure works against this reengineering so we must develop institutions and social reinforcements that inculcate in people the quest for the meaningful self. Throughout our lives, we will be challenged by the existing order to forsake this quest because what currently exists feels so natural and thus so alluring and has been with us for so long. But if we are to break the cycle of illusion perpetuation, we must forward the cause and right of the individual to develop his/her own true beliefs, and these beliefs must be based on reason and be free of illusory influence.

The Implications of a More Rational World

Identifying that illusions do in fact exist and that they have contributed substantially toward our current social malaise is a monumental step in eradicating the distinct set of problems they present. As it is for alcoholics, we cannot eliminate a problem until it is admitted that one exists. With respect to illusions, we must remember they are often so hidden, so imperceptible, that they camouflage their own existence and thus greatly retard the development of any corrective action. As a prudent course, then, we must be ready to confront illusions whenever and wherever they appear. They must be constantly challenged if we are to live free and unencumbered by illusory influence, and we must be resolute in our pursuit of truth.

We must always be mindful that not everyone shares in the quest for a more accurate interpretation of reality; in fact, much of our society ridicules the search for increased meaning and resorts to the disparagement of individuals who pursue this goal, often labeling such people as flakes and misfits. As a result, whenever we encounter someone who is proceeding down the path of growth that challenges illusory influence, we must glorify their efforts and encourage them to go even further in their journey. Whenever one of us transcends illusory influence and creates for ourselves a more realistic interpretation of the life experience, we all benefit.

What might the world be like without illusory influences? We can only speculate, but certainly the world would be more realistic and would, of course, be ruled less by fear. There would be a much greater appreciation for the value of each day. Perhaps the world would be a more considerate place to live as people more realistically understood the importance of all life, not only their own. Children would have greater confidence and this would allow them to exploit opportunities much earlier in life; it would undoubtedly encourage greater academic achievement since children would naturally associate higher levels of knowledge with increased opportunity, and therefore they would embrace learning as a fundamentally important "me" activity that promised real "me" returns.

If we reduced illusory influences, the family would surely benefit. There are very few things as destructive as a dysfunctional family and if we could reduce false conceptions about what a family is and replace it with a more functional model, then adults as well as children would benefit tremendously. Moreover, we could eliminate role playing, a highly illusory state of being, and replace it with a functional structure for the entire family; in short, the family would become a real support team for all of its members instead of the all-to-familiar competitive struggle between conflicting wills.

DISILLUSIONMENT

A more rational and less illusory world has huge sociological implications. Consider, for instance, an economic example: we base much of our fiscal and monetary policies on econometrics which are largely unproven or invalid; as Peter Drucker has noted in *The New Realities*, econometric models are largely invalidated by the theory of complexity, which states that completely accurate forecasts are impossible in complex systems like an economy. But does this fact stop economists in trumpeting their own cause? Of course not. The law of complexity is largely disregarded and instead replaced with economic boasts and proclamations from economists who know essentially very little about the future course of economic events.

Now, if we replaced the illusion of what is economically possible with what is economically achievable, we might be able to instill greater confidence in consumers since they would, perhaps for the first time, comprehend what the limitations are and shift toward a reliance on their own judgements. To glorify our current economic forecasting and interpretive abilities in the face of humiliating recessions and economic hardship is not only ridiculous, but causes a tremendous lack of trust. Moreover, such a professed capability serves to maintain the external directedness of our culture and exists largely for the preservation of power. The focus on improvement within an environment of limitation inspires confidence and would do much to improve consumer attitudes and productivity; the opposite, claiming to have the answers and having time disprove you, destroys faith in the economy and in those who lead it.

Although I have provided some seemingly unrelated examples of how a more rational outlook might impact us sociologically by examining the family and the economy, if we look deep enough we can see that there are connections whenever illusion is replaced by reason; the combinations throughout the sociological spectrum are too numerous to quantify, and as more of these combinations are tried, the total amount of reason in the system will increase and create an accelerative environment for further productive combinations. This invariably becomes one of the primary goals: to cause reason to proliferate to the point that the reduction of illusions eventually leaves more rational and compelling alternatives for consideration.

We are all threatened by the state of disillusionment. Moreover, it is in everyone's interest to eliminate illusory influence and live more rationally, even for those who are threatened by the liberation of people in pursuit of this goal. Why? Because the force of the progress we make sweeps up everyone and benefits all, and most importantly increases the quality of life beyond even those exalted "ruling" positions of today.

Recognizing that we have all been limited through illusory influences in our quest for personal development says much about the current state of disillusionment and how to combat it. In addition, there is much promise in such a cognizance. If we can begin to see how we can remove the barriers of the current system, then we can begin to understand how we might create the proper environment to facilitate our personal and sociological growth. We, then, have arrived in this study at the next stage of our development: understanding.

4
Understanding

As we begin to comprehend how illusory influences have contributed toward our state of disillusionment, we can use our increased reason to understand why this has occurred and how to combat it. Moreover, we can complement our reason with intuition and experience. The combination of reason, intuition, and experience allows us to better understand the nature of reality and to develop a framework for future understanding that can facilitate our now improving journey through life. Understanding without benefit, then, serves no purpose.

The cultural benefit of understanding lies in the ability to discard illusory influences and to avoid repeating mistakes of the past; in addition, social understanding allows for the improvement of all of society's components over time since they are all related, as an improved understanding of one enlightens understanding of the others. The interrelatedness of all the elements within society ensures that merely attempting to clarify or understand one of them will yield increased understanding for the whole.

Understanding sheds light on previous thought. As a result, understanding allows for new ways of looking at things and for the creation of options, both for people and for their society. Understanding opens up possibilities and reduces narrow-mindedness, because understanding is itself a diverse process and cannot be locked in to any one position. Understanding changes and seeks to change, and is never the same for any two people or for any two cultures. And as the sum of the world's knowledge increases, understanding will also increase and change.

As a result, at any particular time we must live with limited knowledge and therefore with less than total understanding. A state of omniscience is an unrealistic possibility for us, certainly never to be expected, although the quest for it is highly desirable since such a quest inevitably increases the sum of the world's reason. This bodes well not only for the reduction of illusory influences, but also for an increase in our intuitive abilities.

Obviously, understanding is a very hopeful process since it creates much opportunity as we progress through life. Moreover, understanding feels good, analogous to those times when one discovers the logic and meaning behind some mathematical problem that has been especially troubling and that has just been solved for the first time. Remember that feeling? There was both relief and a belief in one's future capability. Ability equals confidence.

What Is Understanding?

What then is understanding? More than anything else, understanding is a process. It is the process of learning more about the nature of reality, more about ourselves, and more about our place within that reality. Understanding requires an acceptance of our limitations and a belief that our wisdom must be a Socratic wisdom, which recognizes that we are wise only in the recognition of our ignorance. Understanding knows that an acceptance of our limitations can occur only when we live without fear and eliminate the need to protect against our ignorance. Understanding also knows that personal insecurity limits wisdom, and that a lack of confidence confines us to only that knowledge which can be found within a comfort zone delimited by our own fear.

To accept that understanding is a process, essentially diametrical to our familiar beginning/end frame of reference, can be a difficult realization indeed; to pursue understanding requires a mental paradigm shift toward the awareness of a forward motion without culmination and toward a belief in a continuum that we can progress along, but that never reaches a destination. Until we accept that understanding is a process, we cannot begin to understand.

This is not to imply that the process of understanding is driftless; on the contrary, it is most purposeful and directed. Although we cannot be sure of what we will learn and thus understand, we can be confident that we will know more than we knew before we started and that we are progressing further toward our own potential, but only if we can accept that knowledge without understanding is useless. Once we know this, we have direction, purposeful and meaningful, and we also know that this process is evolutionary and therefore natural. Moreover, we can see, given the evolutionary relevance, that both people and societies are dynamic organisms that evolve over time and that a key to survival is to recognize the importance of understanding.

One can make a strong case that people and nations often fail because they do not understand what is happening to them. For all other species, survival is more or less devoid of choice because there is an inherent lack of reason. But people are different; our ability to reason and to tap into our intuitive sense affords us the opportunity to change the path of evolution, to direct our part in it, and to hopefully create for ourselves a higher probability of success. This is why the elimination of fear and the illusory influences that often result from it are so critical to our prospects for survival; if we can eliminate fear, then what remains is understanding; the process of understanding is how we can best safeguard our futures.

It is only because of our previous frame of reference, i.e. we must have a destination in order to start a journey, that we fail to be more fully appreciative of our path of progress and how this path can increase understanding. When we can appreciate, as part of our heightened sense of reality, that the journey can be directed and meaningful, then we can begin to benefit from the liberation that this recognition allows. Moreover, we will be, for the first time, in a better position to realize the merits of process versus destination and how process invariably leads to better choices.

Understanding, then, is the recognition that the path is the way toward further understanding. We must also accept that our nation is on a path, as is the entire world, and that hopefully it will be the path of understanding and not the path of a hubris that leads to our extinction. We must know that humans form and create that path and that understanding is thus the termination of any form of predeterminism and external directedness.

Understanding must also be the process of liberation from expectations, for the path of understanding is not predetermined, but remains forever changing. The path of understanding can be who we are and it is the road that we can travel. The greater our ability to reduce fears, illusory influences, and our insecurities, the greater will be the level of our self-awareness and our comprehension of reality. At any point along this path, we are certain of not only more understanding, but also of an improved quality of life that a life of choices naturally produces.

Understanding and Quality of Life

When we increase our understanding, we begin to see that the creation of options is a truly human possibility and applicable to everyone; as a result, understanding disposes us toward an awareness of the interrelatedness of people and of the intricate connections that form the full panoply of the humanly possible. Once we see this, we become respectful of everyone's right to choose, and we encourage the self-responsibility inherent in such choices because such behavior is self-rewarding; in short, the support of human choice works to our personal advantage because such support ensures that we will safeguard our right to choose over time. Through this understanding, it becomes evident that the full spectrum of human choice increases the probability of an enhanced life for everyone since everyone benefits through a collective promotion of individual freedom and responsibility.

To increase our quality of life, we must first understand the significance of every life, our own and that of others as well. Why? The connection is simple: quality of life increases proportionally to the degree of responsibility that we individually assume because within an environment of increased self-responsibility, the collective becomes less of a burden through its increased self-corrective abilities. When people act responsibly, and if society develops "training" vehicles to teach people how, then there will be less people that must be "taken care of." If everyone acts more responsibly, the aggregate level of responsibility increases and becomes a sociological improvement mechanism that rewards responsible behavior and discourages irresponsibility.

It is almost ironic that we may be entering a period of social development where an improvement in the quality of life results from an increased self-responsibility that is mandated on the system because we can no longer afford irresponsibility. In short, we can no longer pay for the alternative to acting irresponsibly, especially given the increasingly competitive nature of the global marketplace.

We must understand what is at stake. If we lose the global competition, capitulating our leadership role because of our incompetence, then inevitably our quality of life will diminish. Only through understanding, really seeing our limitations as well as our potential, can we overcome a trend which now appears to demonstrate that we are losing our preeminence. Only through understanding can we first maintain and then improve our quality of life.

Understanding, Powerlessness, and Responsibility

Responsibility for one's own life is the most powerful choice we can make, and this choice opposes in a very fundamental way much of the individual powerlessness that results from fear and disillusionment which we have discussed earlier. Responsibility mandates a reevaluation of our mindset and challenges what we believed had been our security by suggesting power where we had previously believed we were powerless.

Understanding, then, is also partly the realization of the linkage between our responsibility and our conception of ourselves. We will not have a full self-concept until we accept our individual responsibility toward ourselves and toward our society. When we make this association, we increase our internal-directedness and make ourselves more powerful than we were before.

Understanding inexorably increases self-confidence because understanding allows us to know ourselves, and people who know themselves feel more secure. We might say that these people are more powerful, for indeed they are. Although we will discuss power in a subsequent chapter, we can briefly here examine the relationship that power has to understanding and responsibility.

Whether we are the exceptionally gifted person or the average one, we have a responsibility to develop our own power to its fullest extent. Again, if everyone strives to maximize their potential through their individual understanding, everyone benefits since the sum of understanding increases and so does the resulting power of both people and their societies.

Let's look at a brief example. There has been much written about the Japanese economic miracle (recovery) in the post World War II period. Why did this occur? There are innumerable reasons, but one must certainly be the homogeneity of their culture. This is not a supportive argument for racial singularity, but rather for a like-mindedness that works toward a common goal. The Japanese clearly understood what they were up against, and they developed a national directive to accomplish their vision; in short, by combining individual responsibility with understanding, they developed power.

How do we do this? The new individualism must seek to more fully develop the relationship between understanding, responsibility, and power; this will fundamentally mitigate the personal and collective underachievement that results from a powerlessness rooted in fear, and will also do much to overcome individual and cultural disillusionment through an enhanced vision of the future.

Understanding and Illusions

Now we must ask ourselves why we do not have more understanding. We must ascertain what has caused the retardation of our understanding and then develop methods to overcome this deficiency. We have already alluded to the relationship between fear and understanding, especially how the former can hinder the development of the latter. But we have not yet discussed how illusions rooted not only in our fear, but also in our unmindfulness, can circumvent our efforts at understanding reality and accepting our responsibility. In short, we must explore that part of our culture's influence that promotes the status quo through a general complacency among its members and how this complacency inhibits understanding.

Insidiously, our culture fails to promote self-awareness through a sort of benign continuance of shared values that ultimately conditions the individual toward a general conformity. We have already established that this conformity results in part from the belief in the superiority of others and a lack of confidence in the self. But there is also a type of reverence for past ways, really tradition, that impedes the development of understanding. This tradition can be a type of illusory cultural ethos that is not malevolent or promoted by the self-serving ways of some political or cultural elite, but rather develops naturally from the inherent human drive to respect what has preceded us. We all know that we are partly our past, and it is therefore natural to respect, even preserve, what we have been. But whether we promote the status quo from fear or respect is largely irrelevant if the prevailing ethos perpetuates illusion. Understanding must look deeply, sometimes more deeply than we ever imagined possible, if we are to "weed out" illusory influences and increase our comprehension of reality. There are certainly many personally and socially impairing myths pervasive in our culture and we must be wary of all of them.

As an example of one of these myths, let's look at the "higher order" syndrome which implies that things are the way they are for a good reason and that the status quo is a by-product of either God's will or certain biological structures and hierarchies that resulted from the evolutionary process. In either case, the result is to preserve, even encourage, the dominance of an "other" relative to the self, an external power versus an internal. Typically, in the example cited here, the argument is between religion and science over who was behind the creation of the higher order and not the effects of that order on the individual. But either way, people lose. Understanding seeks instead to ask is the "higher order" real or "could there be something else?" Understanding thus seeks to create alternative ways of looking at things to eliminate the "boxes" that we put ourselves in. Understanding reality threatens the status quo and all of the illusion contained within. The single largest illusion that such an understanding of reality destroys is the belief that others are more knowledgeable, more experienced, and more deserving than we are to lead and determine the future course of humankind. One has only to examine the political and economic morass of our culture to understand how inaccurate and destructive this illusion is. The indictment against the stewardship of the external is overwhelming; the "other" framework has had its time and it has not worked for most people.

The Extent of Our Need to Understand

In order to be successful, at least on a scale capable of changing society, we must understand the deeply-rooted, insidious nature of the social forces that work contrary to individual understanding. Of course, not all social forces oppose individual understanding, but because there are some that do, we must see these for what they are and develop strategies to overcome them.

The extent of our need to understand is paramount in this quest; we must understand how firmly entrenched are the social forces which prohibit true understanding, not only those based on obvious illusion, but on ostensible logic as well. When we seek to truly understand, we must see that we are going against the grain of an entire system, and that this system contains many rational, even scientific, elements in its defense; as a result, these social forces assume added credibility and are therefore very difficult to confront.

As an example, consider the role of education in our society. We have been told, for a very long time, that education is the key toward empowering our people and making us globally competitive; in addition, education has been heralded as the way toward overcoming many domestic problems, from drug abuse to poverty to racism. This argument appears logical, and there have been numerous "scientific" studies to support this thesis. The dollars spent in pursuit of our educational policies are astronomical and yet they have failed miserably to achieve their intended goals. Why? Because no one has really understood the extent of the problem. We try to solve our social problems within a narrow band of acceptance, within a "thinking" that considers a limited amount of options or that is possible only within the boundaries of a political system designed to first get votes, not solutions. If people, because of their fear of change and the unknown, vote for candidates and positions within a range largely determined by the status quo, we cannot win. We are then prisoners to our system, limited to choices within an existing framework that forever condemn us to failure because the solution lies outside the system, outside our normal way of looking at things.

To further the above example, education has failed and yet continues to be promoted as the panacea to our nation's ills. Education may work in combination with something else, but it does not work alone. We try to reform the educational system through more discipline, changed curriculums, and vouchers, but the answer to our educational problems lie in something other than education itself, and this innovative course is not pursued.

Until we challenge all of our personal and social assumptions we have no hope of building a better tomorrow. The extent of our need to understand is simply the full extent, to hold nothing as sacred, to see nothing as beyond inquiry and to challenge everything.

The Hope of Understanding

The phenomenon of understanding as we have defined it here is universal, for individuals, groups, societies, and nations are capable of comprehending its definition and its implications. The phenomenon of understanding is everywhere the same; only the degree to which people understand and the timing of their understanding are specific, and in no way does either of these violate the general framework or its applicability. This fact alone causes much optimism and hope since society can be seen as a collection of individuals who are fully capable of understanding themselves by questioning all assumptions and their own relationship to the collective whole.

The progression of human understanding, however, is not completely linear, since there are times when understanding is temporarily derailed by whatever forces oppose it. Our sociological goal, therefore, should be to buttress the efforts to understand against the constant threat of fear and ignorance. We must, as a people, support in all fields the attempts to understand and fight efforts that are set against growth, for this growth causes the requisite changes that ultimately lead to understanding. Understanding at the sociological level, then, is the progression of reason toward the day when individuals live their lives freely, without fear and disillusionment, knowing that tomorrow will bring further discoveries and an improvement in the quality of their lives because people who understand are confident in their total responsibility and welcome making their own choices.

The hope of understanding encompasses the full extent of the human potential in all of its forms. Since the dawn of our species, we have tried to understand our world and develop meaning for our lives in the limited amount of time that we have here. It may be natural that a system of external-directedness evolved, and that humans, because of their fear, capitulated their responsibility or failed to develop it to the necessary extent. But we don't have to accept that reality now. The hope of understanding is that through understanding we can take steps to direct ourselves in more meaningful ways, and in ways that also significantly improve the human condition so that all of humankind can prosper.

The hope of understanding is above all a choice, a choice that we can make to reduce illusory influence, disillusionment, and hopelessness. So far in this book, we have discussed the reality of choices and how these choices, really options, can do much to liberate our spirits and unleash our creative energies. We have the option to improve our quality of life simply by choosing; if living is really all about choice, we have no excuse, except for our fear, not to make the choice of choice.

The Limits of Understanding

Ironically, we must first set the limits of understanding if we are to embark upon any successful attempt to increase our level of understanding and improve our world. We must also know that perfect understanding is impossible and that understanding is first and foremost a process. Understanding is therefore also the reconciliation of the ideal with the attainable and it is fundamentally an acceptance of limitations. We must accept less than the full extent of the hoped for because there exists an insurmountable time constraint: we simply will not live long enough to see many of our dreams fulfilled. But this realization can never circumvent the goal, for the goal is a most worthwhile aspiration as it promises much for the entire human family throughout time; in short, our attempts at understanding can be not only our legacy, but also our gift.

What can be realistically attained? How do we ensure that our reach can exceed our grasp within a realistic framework? We first need a vision, defining what is possible and what should be sought within reason. We must know when to push and when further pushing will yield only frustration and deprive us of necessary energy in the drive toward the attainment of realistic objectives. There are naturally limits of time and space to be considered, as well as questions of energy and inertia.

The goal of understanding is to maximize the fulfillment of the living experience within the realm of the possible. To do this, we must set our own limitations through an acceptance of our individual skills, motivations, and possibilities. Foremost, we need an open mind that is amenable to change, but that is sufficiently capable of valuing truth above all else, regardless of the pain that must be endured in pursuit of that truth. If we have preconceptions that are adhered to after they are proved invalid, or if our fear is too great, the individual can progress no further. We must accept these times when fact is presented contrary to our suppositions, and we must accept these facts even when they offer less than the desired outcome.

Sociologically, we must see the big picture; we must understand our special role in the world and the significance of our nation's history, and we must understand the risks for all of humanity if we as a people lack vision. We must begin to use a more systemic approach that considers the interrelatedness of all of the world's possibilities and we must seek to establish patterns in their relations to make sense of an ever-increasing complexity. We must see understanding as a delightful process, and that our efforts, in combination with the efforts of others, can produce an almost continually synergistic result. We must also see the connection of our predecessors and of our progeny to ourselves if we are to fully develop the most effective vision of the world's future. There is no macro too big or any connection too small. We must understand that this reasoning facilitates our benevolent stewardship of our home, the Earth, and by definition requires the safeguarding of our planet, for only by preserving our planet can we someday pursue its possibilities.

We must also be aware that understanding produces new responsibilities and challenges, and that we must be proactive in our outlook and our approach if we are to be successful. Too often people equate progression with the reduction of challenge; this is inaccurate and facilitates disappointment in the individual. Correctly viewed, progression produces new challenges which, when successfully managed, produce even newer and more difficult ones. This, however, dovetails nicely with our internal sense of direction since the forward motion of understanding matches the innate drive in us that forever prods us to seek new ground and to want more than we have; the drive to excel and the drive to understand are essentially one and the same. The process of understanding plays well into the natural motion of evolution, for it crystallizes the self-preservation motive and the biological imperative to improve the species.

Within this light, understanding necessitates cooperation and compassion toward our fellow human beings in the desire to make the benefits of understanding available to others so that they may be enriched in their own living experiences and thus elevate the aggregate capabilities of humankind. This "elevation" does much to improve our species' survivability rate. Moreover, it provides the necessary environment for the continual improvement of the human condition through the creation of a fertile ground in which the common interest of all can flourish.

Understanding and the New Individualism

To understand, or more correctly to possess a framework of understanding, we must first empathize with the entire human condition and fully comprehend the preciousness of each individual life; we must also recognize the tragedy of lives that are dominated by fear. We must be responsible for our own being, understanding that our courage to live without fear, in a state of freedom, is an example for others to follow; moreover, we do this knowing that living such an existence is both simultaneously individually self-interested and socially beneficial.

To really understand is to reject as many illusory influences as possible and to recognize how our misconceptions limit the scope of human freedom and choice. We must accept, without fail, that our lives are existential and that they are what we make of them; progress and the march of human freedom, what is really meaningful existence, is ours to determine and ours alone.

Understanding is thus the creation of meaning and is a creation of our own choosing. The responsibility inferred here is more than awesome, it is reality exposed. In the final analysis, this is the depth of understanding, that we are what we make of ourselves and that reality and truth are ours to behold. When we attempt to define understanding, to really know what it is to be aware, what we are really referring to is the responsibility for oneself; we must possess the knowledge that the progression of humanity and the results of our labors, such as our cities, our artworks, our languages, our technology, our literature, our knowledge, and our dreams for the future, are all by-products of our responsibility and our drive to succeed.

All of our human successes are created by us; we are responsible for their creation, and the future course of our development, in all of its forms, will be ours to determine as well. Fundamentally, we are creators. Understanding is thus also that process whereby we differentiate and select, through our responsibility, the future course of our species. Could there be a higher form of creation? No other living organism that we know of has this power. And through this power, we not only determine individual outcomes, but collective ones as well. A society, after all, is simply a collection of individual wills, and the responsibility for ourselves is a responsibility for all.

The Threat to an Advanced Understanding

Irresponsibility and ignorance will extinct the species, so the quest for understanding is not only a goal, but an imperative. If we cannot understand reality, if we cannot accept the tremendous responsibility that we have toward ourselves and our planet, and if we cannot contemplate the relation between present action and future course to it's fullest extent, then there is an excellent chance that the human family will not survive. Many would argue that this is overreactive at best, paranoid at worst. These critics, however, fail to understand the full extent of the span of time and how relatively limited is the human experience. We are incredibly vulnerable as a species, with the forces of history, time itself, working against our preservation as it has for the vast majority of all living things. Over 99 percent of the world's species throughout time have gone extinct. To understand our limits and the constraints of our knowledge and technological progress is vital if we are to survive. To know that there are no teleologics, and thus no pre-determined favorable outcomes, is to accept that technology may not always remedy our destructive actions and tendencies; for those who would argue that technology will inevitably save us, we can counter that so far no one has yet devised a method of replacing the ozone layer or curing AIDS or preventing war. Can we really afford to proceed with the assumption that we can always bail ourselves out? To make this assumption is to live in peril, with no guarantee that tomorrow will provide a solution for the problems created today. Such an attitude is a rejection of our responsibility and a vote for the limitation and constraint of the human potential through our own ignorance.

We have already established that life's one constant is change. For better or for worse, the future will bring dramatic changes for which we must be prepared. The most constructive preparation is a realistic worldview, one which seeks understanding through acceptance of our limitations and the value of every individual life.

How do we accommodate our humanity juxtaposed with the forces of change? How does the human remain human in the face of greater psychological demands? What if the biological evolutionary engine fails to converge and meet our challenges?

Actually, the gap between what we need to know and our capabilities has reached crisis proportions, with the need to develop a realistic understanding absolutely critical to our future survivability. This is why we need a new individualism that emphasizes reason and possibility. We must face up to our responsibility, embrace it, and make it universal if we are to successfully meet the challenges ahead, and we must accept that it will require all to participate. We cannot afford to let a segment of our society lag in this endeavor, for their sheer numbers could destroy all that those who accept their responsibility try to create.

If we do not develop this capability soon, on a widescale, then the gulf between the capable and the incapable may prove unbridgeable; the ranks of the incapable will swell and their mass will prove to be unmanageable by those who understand. An-

UNDERSTANDING

other important, indeed vital, component of understanding must be the realization that the numbers of aware people must increase if humanity is to successfully incorporate all of its members. The push for understanding must extend to the collective, it must be more than a realization of the enlightened few, for if it is not, we cannot succeed.

This is why it appears that the new individualism is a social necessity and must be implemented if the human family is to survive. Society is moving at an blistering pace and we must adapt, and quickly, with a new understanding of how our species can meet these and other challenges.

Lastly, the fundamental tenet of the new individualism must be that people have the responsibility to choose what is best for them and that through this choice people answer the call of self-preservation. If we fail to facilitate this responsibility, we are saying that people are not capable of making choices and determining their own futures. We are condemning the majority of humanity to subservience, toward a master who thinks and makes choices for us; through our reluctance to be powerful, we are resigning ourselves to an external directedness that every day threatens our very survival. We deserve more than that, for it is we who have forged the path that brought us here, through a will and a spirit, however fearful and underdeveloped, that longed for something better than we had, and it is we who will move forward toward that place of our own creation that is more of who we want us to be.

5

Excitement

When we begin to understand that we have lived our lives influenced by illusion and limited by fear, we can start to experience a strong sense of excitement for what the future might hold. We come to believe more in our potential. Of course, such a realization is extremely invigorating, energizing, and even powerful. Moreover, there can be much optimism in the awareness that we are growing in our understanding of ourselves and that, for the first time, we have the power to determine the future course of our own lives. For our purposes, however, excitement is even more than that. Excitement is more than an attitude, it is a state of being resulting from an increased awareness and a growing sense of opportunity that ultimately serves as the fuel for our engine of change and growth. Excitement is novelty and discovery, as well as imagination and hope, and is also when the grandeur of being confronts daily routine and forces us to ponder the range of what might be; moreover, it is that time when we are most ourselves, full of life, and yearning for more. It is those periods in our lives when we are in a flow, as Mihaly Csikzentmihalyi has noted in his book *Flow-The Psychology of Optimal Experience,* when we are maximized and congruent with our spirit, for during these times we know we are at our best and we feel passionate and enthusiastic.

Excitement as the Enemy of Fear

When we think of living exciting lives, we can easily understand how excitement facilitates possibilities and encourages the consideration of options; moreover, we have already seen that such a state of being fundamentally opposes fear. Fear is the reduction of possibility, while excitement is the inclusion of what is possible.

Remember the times when we have lived energetically or excitedly; there was a corresponding diminishment of fear because there simply wasn't time to be fearful, and we had more confidence, not only in our abilities, but in the situation as well. Excitement, therefore, allows for a much greater range of options and outcomes because of our willingness to keep moving forward and where fear has even less chance of stopping our momentum.

But the experience of excitement is not limited to individuals. Whenever a state of excitement exists, whether it be for a small group, a corporation, a government, or a nation, there is an intensity of experience where action supersedes hesitation. As an example, think of how a corporate organization looks and feels when its people are excitedly pursuing their tasks, confident in their abilities and the outcomes of their efforts; now think of a corporation in which the people are fearful, afraid to take risks, and are resigned to the drudgery of job duties aimed not for dynamic improvement, but done rather for the sake of not offending and conformity.

Picture a dynamic nation, excited by the prospects for the future. Think of countries that are immersed in the possibilities, where their economies are fueled by people who take risks and who believe in a strong and purposeful vision of themselves and their culture. Some of the developing countries of Asia come to mind, for instance Thailand, South Korea, Hong Kong, and Singapore; to some extent, so does Mexico and the developing nations of Latin America. These nations know that they live in exciting times and that there is much promise in their efforts, and they are focused and purposeful in their mission because they have the belief that what they are doing matters. Their leaders seem excited by the prospects at hand, you can sense the enthusiasm in their messages, and through their confidence they inspire their people. Moreover, we in America are often enamored with their success, it reminds us of how we used to be, and we are envious of the passionate spirit that lives in other places of the world.

But why isn't America more like these dynamic countries? Why don't we have more of the same optimistic spirit?

Some would say that it is simply an economic fact of life, that emerging economies have an inherent advantage because they have so much building to do; in short, the argument is one of developing economy versus mature economy. We simply cannot be energetic and excited about the future because we've already been there and lived it, and now it is our time to watch others have theirs. Of course, there is the usual rhetoric of how we encourage these global developments to open up markets for our products, but there is the absence of any real talk regarding why we don't have more of the fire or the passion to dramatically improve our futures relative to these emerging nations.

In truth, we are afraid we will fail. We are afraid to risk, to try to move beyond the "mature capitalist economy" phase of economic development into a new tomorrow. It is easy to stay where we are; we're already there. But if our nation is to prosper, to ensure that our quality of life is increased, we must take risks that lead to more exciting possibilities. If we don't risk, every successive American generation will have less opportunity than the previous one; we are already witnessing this throughout our culture. And, in order to be successful, this risk-taking must include the consideration of all options at our disposal.

We must also trust in our ability to measure risk, to take risk in stride, and to constantly weigh how much benefit is acceptable given some level of risk; we do this all the time in management and economics, but we must do it for our culture as well. Rarely does anyone formulate a risk-benefit analysis for our society at large, to really evaluate how we could take chances to increase our national level of production or happiness. Is there any doubt that this would be an exciting exercise that could yield almost incalculable results?

It is not necessary, however, that we undertake some elaborate risk/benefit mathematical model ahead of every contemplated action, but instead that we should rely on a combination of empirical and sensible abilities to recommend more exciting courses of action whenever possible, and that we ought to consider a wider framework than what is generally accepted or known. Such a framework will enable us to develop an ever-growing sense of self-security that reduces fear and maximizes our possibilities.

Excitement has another effect on fear: whereas fear causes anxiety and worry, excitement increases confidence and ability. Increased confidence in our abilities almost invariably leads to greater appreciation and gratitude for what we have done and for future possibilities. In this way, excitement contributes toward a more positive outlook since it disposes us to a thankfulness for what we have accomplished while simultaneously causing us to want more. Confidence typically encourages further risk-taking, more reward, and more desire for reward. This in turn causes us to achieve more, and the more we achieve the more we subsequently appreciate what we have accomplished; this produces even more confidence, more risk-taking, more reward, and more desire for reward. Soon, we are in an extremely positive spiral leading us to greater levels of accomplishment and happiness.

As we have seen, fearfulness produces a lack of initiative which causes a lack of diversity. Excitement, however, has the opposite effect for it increases diversity and exposure to different things thereby making life more interesting and creative. Excitement, then, mitigates boredom by reducing the amount of patterned behavior and replacing it with variety. It is probably fair to say, then, that diversity and variety contribute not only to lessening boredom, but to building a foundation for creating future excitement that minimizes the likelihood that self-limiting patterns of behavior will appear.

The Phenomenon of Excitement

For many people, life has become a dull and unchallenging proposition. One of the most troubling trends in this regard is the "graying" of America, since our culture tends to "put out to pasture" many of our senior citizens who often complain that life has become listless and without purpose; there are also many people who fall into this "directionless" life who are not elderly. Certainly, however, there is an underlying and very potent social mental model that reinforces the belief that with aging comes a corresponding reduction in inspired alternatives; this cultural mindset is clearly built into our value system. Fortunately, it is untrue. Nowhere does it state that life mandates some inexorable change toward sedation or that we must become in some way desensitized to living passionately as we advance in years or in our careers.

We must recognize the need to make our lives more exciting in order to increase our productive capacity in all of our citizens, especially our older ones; bored, aging citizens become a tremendous financial burden on those who must support them, and non-productive citizens are an albatross around our collective necks. What our culture must do, however, is to show our population the way to be productive throughout their lives by demonstrating what the exciting possibilities of life can be. We must stop those who join the ranks of the non-productive before they reach their later years due to disillusionment or fear because they only add to an already overstrained system, and coupled with the aging of our population they will prove catastrophic to our society. We must stop the "dispassionism" of our people before it stops us.

Life itself does not get uninspiring; the reason life appears so is our inability to make life exciting, and until we accept our responsibility toward building our own excitement, we have little chance of success. There is nothing more fundamental to making our lives more exciting than the acceptance of this responsibility since life, being itself indifferent, will not provide excitement on its own.

What does the phenomenon of excitement mean for our lives? It means a higher quality of life and one that is value-added over time. As we proceed with increased excitement in our living experience, we gain more from the other aspects of our existence since excitement heightens the senses and increases our motivation to be successful in all that we do. In short, excitement produces synergistic results at every stage of our development because excitement increases combinative possibilities and the drive to pursue them, while simultaneously providing the rewards necessary to encourage similar behavior.

When we live more exciting lives, we dramatically improve the quality of life for the people that we know and influence; this includes family, friends, work associates, or virtually anyone that we interface with. Excitement is contagious. Others can see that we do more with our time and enjoy it more, and they naturally want to participate in a similar lifestyle. Now imagine what the world would look like if everyone led more exciting lives and influenced others to do the same. Wouldn't the cumulative effect, what we might refer to as global passion, produce incredible opportunities for the human family? Isn't there a good chance that through this collective energy and excitement we could successfully tackle many of today's problems, solve them, and build a better system? Wouldn't the quality of each individual life be substantially improved?

We are all running out of time. Most of us want to make sure that in our final years we can reflect back on our lives with an appreciation of how we have lived. If what is being advocated here, increased excitement and opportunity through an elevation of global possibility, is accepted and practiced by people who, through their examples, cause humanity to aspire to new heights, then wouldn't the world be a substantially better place to live?

Wouldn't it be more exciting and fun? Wouldn't we all be making a contribution?

Excitement and Perception

In order to ensure that we don't fall into the trap of believing that life will somehow magically transform itself into a more exciting and satisfying experience without any initiative on our part, we must understand the relationship between perspective and excitement. Given the inescapable fact that there is much repetition in life and that we often "box" ourselves into a narrow range of possibility, we must develop a sense of perception that is hypersensitive to these tendencies. This is not as easy as it sounds for it requires considerable effort on our part, and it also means that the effort must be continuous and ever mindful of our predisposition toward self-limitation.

Most of what we do or how we view things is really perception. If we see things as more exciting, they probably will be. Moreover, if we are directed by a sense that what we perceive is at least partially determined by our own conative processes, then we begin to understand that what we do can, in fact, create excitement simply as a by-product of our action. Excitement can become a larger part of our lives simply by recognizing our role in its creation. Certainly, most of the things that we do, such as our job or how we spend our leisure time, can be reworked, at least mentally, to make them more exciting and more rewarding.

If we have failed in our perception regarding the potential of the human life, or more directly, whether our lives are exciting or dull, it is because our perception of how life is supposed to be is fundamentally flawed. When we see the quality of our lives as something externally directed, we lose the opportunity to create for ourselves a truly enjoyable life. We must change our perception to one emphasizing life's possibilities, and we must recognize that we require an internal focus that shifts the burden toward the development of an exciting life to us and away from something as abstract as life itself.

Awareness of this burden shifting is imperative if we are to change our perception regarding the reality of life and our role in forming this reality. If we do not accept our responsibility for the creation of reality, it will be impossible for an exciting life to truly emerge. If we do not take the responsibility for building a "self" directed framework in which we see ourselves as the sole generator of an on-going life of excitement and promise, we will be forever limited to those few, chance instances in life in which something exciting occurs.

Through our individual efforts, we can do much to change the perception of society. If our society seems somewhat dull, redundant, and uninspiring, it is because we as a people have failed to create the excitement in our own lives that can transfer to the social whole. There are certainly exciting happenings occurring in the world, but we lack a universal belief that posits the full potential of humankind and one that could overcome our impression of the immutability of the system and the innate limitations of its members. If we can change our perception, then we can begin to construct the exciting possibilities that await us.

Excitement and Sociological Conditioning

What things must be changed in order for people to change their perceptions regarding an exciting life and to accept their responsibility for making it happen? What must we do if we are to change this perception in broad measure and create for all of us a better society in which to live? How can we progress to an understanding of how more individually exciting lives can dramatically improve the social experience?

First, we must change our notion, really our collective

worldview, that passivity is preferred over activity and that preservation of the status quo is thought better of than change. We must opt for an activism that seeks to fundamentally alter the system through the efforts of its people, and not wait for the system to change us.

Second, we must stop complaining and strive to create solutions, even to dilemmas previously thought unsolvable. We must go away from a society that feels victimized and toward one that feels "possibilitized" and which seeks answers instead of more unanswerable questions. We must begin to accept that realized potential falls to those who have been wronged and see the future as a chance to right that wrong, and we must also recognize that failure inevitably comes to those who have been wronged and who continually use this fact as an excuse for their inaction. We must stop believing that someone owes us something and start believing that we owe ourselves.

Lastly, we must utilize the full resources at our disposal and advance to areas heretofore deemed implausible. We must utilize what we know and cease to rely on precepts which exist primarily for their comfort or safety. We must insist that our social institutions further our forays into new approaches, discarding programs or agendas that are ineffective and relied upon almost entirely because of their "status quo" status. We must challenge our governmental operating system and replace it with a political body that truly represents the wishes of the people it now only purportedly serves. We must ask more of our corporate culture in fulfilling people's needs and in ensuring that the progression of human self-actualization is at least as important as profits; we must make sure that corporations understand that profit is increased through the efforts of motivated, responsible people. And we must ask more of our families; we must make it incumbent upon the family to create an environment where children can feel the exciting possibilities of life, and where they can dream without the threat of violence, abuse, or abandonment. We must therefore take parenting much more seriously, since through improper parenting our children will not dream or seek exciting possibilities for themselves or for their society.

Excitement and Historical Timing

Skeptics might at this point ask "isn't this extremely idealistic and the possibility of success highly improbable?" "Hasn't this been tried before?" Most assuredly, reform movements have appeared throughout history, but often what was once thought unthinkable or impossible has often become normative. Something is idealistic only until it becomes the standard. To reform society through personal, institutional, or familial change has many historical precedents, some of which have resulted from suddenly increased awareness and some from the gradual progression of history itself that precipitated change as a result of its momentum. We must see our current efforts toward sociological reform as a continuation of this historical process; seen in this light, the movement toward sociological self-correction through personal change is de facto validation that people alone must do it.

The new individualism is itself a by-product of history, a chapter in a book of movements. We cannot separate how the emergence of a new individualism is now being historically demanded from previous change movements, even when these earlier movements seem crude or naive by comparison. In fact, we can see that the creation of more exciting lives is really an extension of a movement started long ago, when humankind first developed the ability to reason and to dream of what might be.

Corollary to this point is the cause and effect nature of what might be called "successive generation theory" on the present. There has been much written and discussed regarding the impact of generations, this being certainly intensified by the huge demographic bulge of the baby-boomers, and there appears to

THE NEW INDIVIDUALISM

be an even stronger impetus for future study of this type since so much of generational theory is extremely relevant for a variety of fields; a good case study of this is the book *The Great Boom Ahead* by Harry S. Dent, Jr.

One of Mr. Dent's major contentions is that every generation eventually comes into its power, through economic/financial achievement or political arrival. Interestingly, as he points out, the massive baby-boom generation is approaching its most impactful time. The power positions, defined as those in society that can have the greatest effect on the greatest number of people, are increasingly becoming available to this generation; this is a generation steeped in individual, corporate, and sociological improvement, and a generation that has always been characterized as self-oriented. The hope is that this "selfness" facilitates a natural amenability toward the new individualism with the result being a formula for some amazing change potential, especially that which concerns individual responsibility, less government, and personal fulfillment.

This in itself is very exciting and has much potential for the furtherance of excitement creation in our society. We must understand that society has matured to the point where real and rapid productive change is virtually certain because of the distribution and networking possibilities facilitated by the Information Age, and we must also understand that we can be the catalyst for such change through our increased self-confidence and commitment to ourselves; this is not only very exciting, but certainly does much to increase our own sense of value as it becomes clearer that we, as individuals, are vitally important to the future of humankind. This is an understanding that is incredibly opportunistic for our species, for we find ourselves at that precise moment in history where our efforts to increase the passion in our lives fuses with the passion required to guarantee our futures.

Whenever the stakes are high there is excitement, and the stakes today are extreme. The human organism must adapt rapidly in such times if the species is to survive. One of these adaptations requires people to become much more aware and much more diversified in their worldview if we are to begin to manage problems that would appear to be now approaching unmanageability. An approach which seeks to use synthesis is absolutely vital to our potential success since most of the solutions will result from some combinative undertaking. This emphasis is particularly exciting since it stresses diversity and generality in its methodologies, and demands that people engaged in the process be more macro in their approach and much more systems oriented. As it becomes increasingly evident that more and more people will be required to have broader knowledge in furtherance of their specialties, we should, once we surmount our fear, become more diverse, more exciting, and more capable.

How do we capitalize on these incredible times? We simply must prepare ourselves for them. This is actually very easy to do if we will make the effort, really committing to improving ourselves and sharing in the vision. We have an absolutely incredible opportunity to make our lives more exciting and fulfilling by exercising our choice toward our individual responsibility, and we have the potential within this choice to cause tremendous sociological change that promises to radically improve the sum of the human experience. History now affords us the chance to construct for ourselves a self-concept and worldview that was impossible for previous generations. The possibilities are absolutely limitless if we will only act to make them happen.

Excitement Creation

What must we do to create excitement? What is the initial step required to make a mental shift toward individual initiative and away from a reliance on others in order that we can do what we must do for ourselves?

THE NEW INDIVIDUALISM

Perhaps the simplest and most effective way to answer these questions is to develop a list of techniques that redirects our energies toward seeking exciting alternatives for our lives. The list is certainly not all-inclusive and represents only a small percentage of what can be done. We must always remember that life is a process, so the framework we create must be process oriented if we are to be in harmony with the basic flow of life. As a result, there are very few quick-fixes and so most of the items on the list require a long-term orientation. The list is as follows:

1. Without clinging to the past, we need to remember the enthusiasm of youth and recall the intensity associated with the discovery of new things. Recognize that we are in a better position as adults to live passionately because we have the experience we lacked in childhood to recognize self-contained and stagnant choices.
2. We should strive to live for today, but also to see how today's choices effect tomorrow.
3. Accept that control is a response to fear, and that when we seek to control we diminish possibilities. Then try letting go. Recognize that it will be scary at first, but that each time we risk we will feel an increase in confidence and self-esteem. Over time, it will become apparent that success will cause us to take additional risks as our confidence grows.
4. All of us need to develop an historical perspective. We need to understand the unique, incredibly rare opportunity that being alive represents in relation to the span of time. We cannot allow this recognition to rush us, but rather must use this awareness to develop more patience.
5. We need to start practicing more diversity and pursue broad-based interests in addition to our specialties.

EXCITEMENT

6. It may sound cliché, but we all need to stop and smell the flowers. We need to understand that although time is precious and we have much to do, enjoyment is also a large part of living.
7. We need to focus more on people and less on things. Human beings are the most intricate and complex creatures of all, as well as the best teachers, so we should strive to surround ourselves with interesting people and friends.
8. We all need to travel more and take in new places. There is much that we can learn about ourselves when we place ourselves in new environments.
9. We must find ways to associate ourselves with the ever-increasing complexity of life and still maintain our perspective. We must embrace possibility and not be intimidated by it.
10. We must develop a greater custodial attitude regarding the Earth. It is sheer tragedy what we have collectively done to our home, and we must take steps to ensure that we safeguard our planet for future generations.
11. We must also read more. One of the great misfortunes of our society is the reliance upon television and cinema for our recreation. More tragic still is that many people rely on these two avenues for metaphysical exploration as well. We need to reevaluate our time allocations for reading and increase them substantially, for we are in a knowledge time.
12. We need to reevaluate the concept of family and what it means, and we need to take more time to appreciate our families and how they contribute toward a well-rounded and satisfying life. We need to challenge existing family roles and promote an atmosphere of individualism and growth within the family structure. This will allow for more diversity and opportunity for all family members and make for a family model that

has more vitality and is more exciting, as well as more supportive.
13. We need to reposition our career framework to focus on the satisfaction to be derived from our labors and not simply the financial or monetary rewards. Employment should be an extension of the self, not something to be done grudgingly in order to pay our bills.
14. We need to support others in their quest for their individualism, and we cannot be threatened by the personal strength of other people. We must see how much benefit there is for us in letting others be strong.

This list is only a start; the rest is up to us. The new individualism will always be an individual undertaking, and the creation of more exciting and fulfilling lives is thus our responsibility as well. Whenever we complain that our lives are lacking in excitement and passion, we have only to look to ourselves for the solution.

Once we understand what the exciting possibilities of life can be, we can use our increased passion to build on other aspects of our characters that have suffered from the fear and disillusionment so evident in our history. Moreover, we can construct for ourselves a society that best fulfills our needs and that allows for us to continually add to our new base. Most importantly, we can develop our own morality and power, and we can use these to advance our understanding and ensure that the process continues. Let's take a look at how we can next.

6
Morality

When we engage the possibilities of life, we must invariably determine what our codes of behavior are and what is to be our concept of right and wrong. As we come to understand more about ourselves, we realize that the principles that direct our lives need to be formulated by us in order for them to hold personal relevance; we know that principles are valid only if they hold validity for us personally since we cannot be loyal to principles in which we lack connection or belief. The search for our principles is a high calling, for without them and without their suitability, we cannot develop a moral life or find a sense of fulfillment or meaning in our lives; to pursue a morality true to ourselves is to tap into our true being, and is a pursuit worthy of our diligence.

Philosophers throughout the ages have attempted to develop moral codes and standards of behavior that were universally valid in an effort to unify and even codify the way humans interacted, usually with some "right" or moral conduct the desired goal. The question of morality has been discussed on both an individual and a societal basis for a very long time; much time, energy, and diligence toward understanding the differences and similarities between individual and collective morality has been, and continues to be, pursued by some of the world's most capable people.

In this pursuit, we as a species have also sought the construction of moral codes that were commensurate with the best interests of people and their society. The purpose, form, and scope of morality has long been a subject of intense debate among nations and there has also clearly never been a universal morality among the peoples of the world; this quest has nevertheless been historically ubiquitous throughout the cultures of the globe. But what is morality and whose is it to determine anyway?

What Is Morality?

Any sociological examination of morality will inevitably fail to yield a universally valid standard of behavior or an all inclusive package of beliefs. There are simply too many issues to be covered and far too many that are widely disputable. Moreover, most philosophical inquiries have been poorly disguised attempts at validating the philospher's own fundamental assumptions, so we can be reasonably certain that there has never been a completely objective examination of the subject. We can, however, explore morality and how it can be studied and made more consensual. In addition, there are many shared values and standards of behavior that are widely adhered to or that have much potential for social cohesion because they are accepted by divergent segments of society, and this provides a hope that some aspects of morality can, in fact, be agreed upon.

Fundamentally, morality is an examination of right and wrong and the manner in which people form guiding principles in order to direct their actions and live their lives. Naturally, morality is a very large part of our mental model and one that provides direction for how we live. We can also infer that if our morality is somehow flawed, based on illusory influences or simple untruths, we might not progress as far as we otherwise might in our own moral development. Moreover, if any one individual can be morally disadvantaged through the socialization process, isn't it logical to assume that society in general could be handicapped as well? Isn't it just as likely that society is hindered through a morality that lacks a wholly rational foundation?

For the purposes of this examination, what is probably most helpful is to explore morality through an understanding of the interrelationship between the individual and society, the effect they have on each other, and the gaps that exist between the two. The point here, which hopefully will be evident soon, is that it is extremely difficult to study morality in a definitive way since so much of our own morality is difficult to distinguish from that of our culture and because the latter is so pervasive and so formative. It is also reasonable to doubt that most people possess awareness of how they might draw the line between moral precepts of their own choosing and those gleaned from social experience. The recognition of this division, if not quite actually a full dichotomy, is not only fundamental to an understanding of this chapter, but also to an understanding of ourselves.

Individual and Collective Morality

At the core, morality is an individual issue that is almost always partially formed by a larger and stronger social structure. Almost invariably, the individual and social moralities come into some kind of conflict, at least on certain issues, since experience alone will mandate that people eventually exercise some moral differentiation due to the lack of moral universality. It is also very difficult to say exactly what a person would morally "buy into" if that person could somehow escape prior moral conditioning. Unfortunately, much of our base moral questioning confronts our predisposition toward fear and as a result many people retreat into the sanctity of the morally familiar; this, in large part, explains why more people do not construct a morality of their own choosing. Quite simply, people are often afraid to do so, and their fear prevents a clear understanding of the role played by sociological influences in their own moral foundations.

When we speak of the formative social effect on our own individual morality, we refer to the process whereby a society promotes a widely held set of values, or perceived to be held, by a majority of the society's members who then forward that morality and seek through that forwarding its continuation over time. One cannot be brought up in a society and not be morally conditioned by it. Moral influence is pervasive throughout society's institutions and governmental structure. To a large extent, this is why we don't feel much differentiation between our two major political parties since their "moralities" are largely the same; neither has often considered moral options outside a narrow window of accepted "American" morality.

Often, the prevailing morality is really the value system of a cultural elite packaged and sold as an accepted social belief. The "majority's" morality, then, thus affects individuals through a social influence that appears to be democratically determined and thus widely ascribed, but that is really propagated by an elitist structure. Within such a system, conformity is revered while dissimilitude is discouraged. This is why the morality of a society is highly "change resistant," for both elites and the majority of society's members adhere to a morality that tends to reinforce one another; if the society begins to drift morally, then the cultural elite will begin to promote the preexisting morality in order to "right the ship." Conversely, if politicians act "immorally," they are voted out of office which has the net effect of negating any leadership that challenges the moral status quo. The "system" is thus self-perpetuating.

If the above seems particularly indicting against social systems, even to the point of appearing to be an advocacy of moral anarchy, let me point out that the issue of moral formulation by individual or collective means is one of degree; certainly, democratic societies are much less likely to wholly morally influence, in an inexorable and complete way, any one individual, than say is a totalitarian system whose moral pronouncements are in reality nothing more than blatant propaganda and mind control. At least in democratic societies, there are occasionally opposing moral opinions and the individual is allowed, to some degree, a moral choice.

There nonetheless remains, however, some similarities in any social system in terms of the cultural influence vis a vis that of the individual. Without question, it is far more likely that a person will be influenced by a prevailing collective morality than the collective will be influenced by the morality of any one individual. It is a rare individual indeed who can influence, to a measurable degree, the morality of the collective. Occasionally, however, we have seen this occur as with Abraham Lincoln or Dr. Martin Luther King, Jr., where a significant transformation of the existing morality is achieved through the actions of one individual.

The Exposure to Hypocrisy

As just mentioned, there is occasionally a fusion of moral influences within our society as when the existing morality incorporates some new moral precept; we must, however, at some point recognize that this is extremely rare and that we are largely morally conditioned through a process much larger than ourselves and one not subject to much singular individual influence. Moreover, we must also see that many of our moral choices are steeped in illusory collective influence and are thus not "real." This awareness is extremely difficult to cultivate and typically begins only with some exposure to hypocrisy, manifesting itself as a "reality check" between our beliefs and our experience.

Hypocrisy thus makes us doubt ourselves, as deceit invariably causes feelings of inadequacy simply because we feel we should have recognized the deception. We therefore start to doubt our own judgement, maybe even believing that our own perceptions are not to be trusted. In future situations, we may find ourselves asking whether we should attempt to trust and we may become calloused, defensive, and skeptical.

This is what has occurred within our body politic; we simply are hesitant to trust our leaders or our own sense of judgement in picking them. Whenever they fall short of our expectations, they not only let themselves down, but us as well. Within our political and corporate leadership resides our sense of judgement, and when our leaders forsake their responsibility to judge well, we incorrectly surmise that we have also judged poorly.

Let me provide a real-life example to illustrate this point. The real tragedy of political scandals such as Watergate or Iran-Contra is the devaluation of our morality resulting from the gap between rhetoric and action, and which creates an incongruity between what we want for our society and what we get; as a result we are out of balance with our sociological setting. We are often shocked and dismayed at the insincerity of our leaders and the gap that exists between their morality and that of our own.

Of course, it doesn't stop there. If we do not have the power to make the offenders change, or at least admit the error of their ways, then we come to recognize our individual inability to effect change on the system and we also become more convinced of our sociological dysfunction; this causes an even further erosion of our own morality and gives rise to social apathy.

Morality is fundamentally related to individual power, which we will see in the next chapter, and it is a truism that any powerlessness limits the creation of a valid moral code. Hypocrisy, especially that evident in the political process, elicits bitter emotional responses and the effects can be extremely enduring and destructive; through an exposure to hypocrisy we may come to doubt our own morality since we come to see it as differing substantially from the larger, social morality of which we previously believed we were a part and to which we have put so much trust. Since we naturally seek to belong, to identify with a larger whole, the compromise of our moral position and the severing of our moral connection with society is felt as a personal loss.

The Effects of Hypocrisy on Individual Morality

But what are the effects of hypocrisy in relation to our individual moral code? What does hypocrisy do to the morality component of our worldview? Can an exposure to hypocrisy actually free us toward the development of our own true moral code, one founded on logic and without illusory influence?

Think of the people you know have been affected, to a significant degree, by hypocrisy. Most are probably cynical and acrimonious, bewildered at the difference between their moral code and the morality of others. As a consequence, many people begin to distrust other aspects of their own morality and they also begin to question their upbringing, their social relationships, and their own thought processes; many times, people begin to wonder whether the balance of their moral code has any legitimacy at all. In short, they begin to question their own foundations, and although painful, such a self-evaluation process is actually beneficial; fortunately, by shaking our foundations, sometimes even crumpling them, we are forced to develop new ones.

This, however, is not true in all cases; because of fear, some people use the hypocrisy of others to justify their own morality which may or may not be (probably not) grounded in reason, and the result is a simple defensive posturing. Obviously, this can be more detrimental to the individual's moral progression than the hypocrisy itself since the individual, owing to the hesitancy to question, remains deceived, stagnant, and closed to the truth. The exposure to hypocrisy can be beneficial for individual growth and change since it allows for conflict resolution and thus moral progress, but we must let it. If we fail to question our own morality, then we cannot change or discard, synthesize or form, new moralities; i.e., we cannot grow morally.

Herein lies the beauty and the necessity of the new individualism, for we, individually, must determine the course and result of our exposure to hypocrisy. Such an exposure will inevitably occur and we must make the most of it. This is why we must foster an environment which allows people to understand that they have this choice, so that when this situation arises they will not abdicate their responsibility and thus reconcile themselves to living a life devoid of moral self-determination.

We must encourage the development of an environment which exposes people to hypocrisy in order to facilitate moral self-determination. If we fail to do this, we run the risk of losing, perhaps forever, large segments of our society who in the current setting lack the security and support for such a monumental mental reworking. We must change the current perception that morality is somehow rigid or basically incapable of much change. We must make the concept of morality more adaptable and more process oriented if we are to create a social milieu where people can freely determine what is in their own moral self-interest. We must create a social climate whereby people feel enabled to make a morality of their own choosing.

Moreover, we must recognize that not everyone capitalizes on an opportunity at the same rate or at the same time. We must fight hard to ensure that an elitist morality does not continue, designed to make moral choices for people in the belief that most of humanity is incapable of making these choices for themselves; true morality must be for everyone, for only people can really say what is best for them. If we trust in the reasonableness of people, we need not fear their moral choices.

Reduced Hypocrisy Through a Changed Environment

Imagine a world where people were taught that morality was an entirely individual undertaking, based on a growing reasonableness as the human family progressed, and that much of what appeared moral was in fact illusory, full of hypocrisy, and a formidable obstacle in the formulation of their own morality. In such a world, where people knew that morality was theirs to create, everyone would strive to ensure that the moral code of society was more representative of their own moral beliefs; the social system's operation would be to first guarantee moral opportunity for all, and people would take steps, even legislate, a morality whose major tenet would be to perpetuate the belief in moral freedom and moral choice for all.

Reality, then, would more likely match our desires and morality would become much more personally fulfilling. Each generation would recognize the opportunity moral freedom represents and would seek to create an ever expanding morality based on reason and truth and that continued such a process over time. We would move toward inclusionary morality and away from the almost incessant moral advocacy which separates our people and divides our nation along moral lines of demarcation.

Morality would become fundamentally self-responsibility, with society being a state where the sum of morality was a compilation of individual moral codes committed first to everyone's right to choose rationally. Morality would be founded on the principle that morality is an individual matter and that everyone has the same opportunity to contemplate moral issues for themselves through an internal, illusory-cognizant self-directedness. We would also know that the morally possible is inexorably linked with the human potential, and that there is never any ultimate moral reality other than the one which guarantees the right that we all have to determine what is moral for us. Our codes of conduct would be based on truths, whatever they may be, with reason, freedom, and choice the guiding principles that direct our lives. Once illusory influences are reduced, reason would predominate and moral advocacy would begin to decrease in frequency because reason unifies. These commitments to individually determined morality would thus become the determinants of our new moral code, one in which society would advance individual progression and freedom of choice and not the perpetuation of moral codes designed by cultural elites to control people and to preserve their power. Gone would be the belief that moral self-expression is a threat to the existing power structure.

The Illusion of a Collective Morality

Throughout human history, there has been a record of various groups or individuals who have sought to use morality as a tool to attain or perpetuate power; invariably, the goal of this morality has been universal application since universality legitimates power. The divine right of kings and the succession of leadership within certain political groups (Mexico and Japan) are but two examples of how morality is perpetuated through an assumed moral universality.

But there have always been counter-groups or contradistinct individuals who sought moral liberation. Human history is thus also the recordation of movements against any morality that cross-purposed true moral legitimacy, which is to say any morality that sought moral subjugation. For those who posit that our American liberal tradition is such a liberating morality, we have to ask why then has it failed to deliver improved moral futures and why has it fueled so much moral advocacy and moral irresolution? Moreover, why do so many people feel morally incongruent with the prevailing social morality? Why do we have a moral social fabric that is undeniably fraying and that is threatening to completely unravel?

Could it be that our society lacks moral cohesion because we have never allowed individuals to take an honest look at their own morality? Could it be that people have never really considered the construction of their own morality because morality has been more or less imposed on them, sometimes purposefully and sometimes from a benign system failure, the result of fear, disillusionment, and perceived lack of choice?

We cannot say that people are immoral or that they lack the capability to construct their own moralities until we give them a chance. Until we stop deciding for them and instead let them choose their own morality, we cannot hope to improve our moral situation. Until we trust people, we cannot trust in their moral abilities.

First, however, we must address the fear of those who say that people are not capable. We must provide the basis on which moral self-determination can be based.

Moral Logic

Individually determined morality is not the same as moral anarchy, or what might lead to anarchy. Naturally, there must be limits to the extension of moral freedom until that time when our species is sufficiently mentally advanced; certainly, there must be some rules to guarantee the safety of individuals and a basic moral doctrine to guide the society until such time. But we must begin the process of morally liberating people so that they can eventually develop this capability. Most of our moral formulations are essentially "natural" anyway, a by-product of reason, and can usually be accepted by anyone who uses logic as their moral prerequisite. Moreover, once fear is reduced the logical element within the moral formulation process assumes greater influence and this will serve to decrease the defensiveness which so typically characterizes moral debate. When we fear less, we will be less likely to take unyielding moral positions.

THE NEW INDIVIDUALISM

The manifest hypocrisy in our society stems more from unreasonableness and ignorance than from any other factors, and these are also typically the characteristics of those people who attempt to determine the morality of others. In short, people are probably more morally capable than the elites who govern or influence them since the elitist position tends to present unmanageable dilemmas (how does one control society's huge number of moral combinations) that do not apply to individuals making their own moral calls. True morality is really not that complicated, but our leaders would often like us to believe that it is. Morality is best advanced through simplicity.

If we can assume that reason is imperative and causative in the development of morality, then we can have hope in a more moral future since humanity possesses a rational capability and this capability is likely to increase in the future. And, if the sum of our reasonableness increases by including larger numbers of people, then an individually determined morality, free of illusory influences, will yield a moral product higher than that constructed through an elitist only position. By allowing people the opportunity to make more of their moral determinations over time, we will do much to increase the quality of our future cultural morality.

Whenever we retard the development of individually driven morality, we increase the hypocrisy in our society. Moreover, moral advocacy leads to what the Clinton administration calls gridlock, and what we, with some additional caveats, can call system inertia. Moral advocacy is the directive, rooted in fear, which most often accounts for the continuation of poverty, warfare, and social inequality in our system since very little gets accomplished when the agenda is who controls what morality.

Perhaps it might be best to provide an example of how unreasonableness can contribute toward a dysfunctional collective morality that can prove especially troubling and persist far longer than what one might rationally expect. Consider the issue of gender in our society. For whatever reason, fear, control, biological difference, or random dysfunction, men have exercised superiority over women, at least in terms of economic opportunity and sociological persuasion. All of our presidents, most of our leading thinkers, and most of our financially affluent have been or are men. Why? Well, what of unreasonableness. Pure stubborn human will, threatened by change, that causes an unyielding morality. And, even though most of us "know" that the genders are basically equal, at least as it relates to the human potential, we tend to allow the disparity to exist. Does it seem reasonable that this occurs? Of course not. But this brief example serves to demonstrate the persistent, even enduring, nature of a morality which, although often challenged, lacks rational support and continues to cause social animosity and acrimony.

So how do we get there? How do we become more rationally moral? We have attempted to show why it is important, but we have not yet discussed the plan itself, the strategy to succeed in our quest for moral self-determination. Moreover, we need to link the path with the goal: that morality is an individual pursuit, and that the individual in this pursuit must rely on his/her reason, even if the advancement of that reason may prove currently inadequate to achieve the full, desired goal. Like virtually everything else discussed in this book, the quest for a rational morality, in a form higher than that which currently exists, is a process. The drive for morality extends along a continuum, with every advance closer to the ideal. In our lifetimes we may never get there, but at every stage, every successive furthering along the spectrum, our lives will be enriched and the probability of even greater success for future generations dramatically increased.

The New Individualism and Morality

The path toward a more rational morality begins with an acceptance, a responsibility, that our individual morality is not only ours to determine, but possible only if internally directed. In addition, the most rational morality is the morality truest to the individual; it is his\her own moral perspective, his\her own moral choice. The way toward rational morality must include determinations as to what is illusory and what is real based on the ability to reason; naturally, it must also include an individual assessment of how morality can be achieved and what is attainable and unattainable.

We must also understand that every individual moral determination must approach the point of a zen; people will become their morality, it is who we are, and what we are will be indeterminable from our morality. The payoff is this: such a synthesis of people and their morality will mean a sharp reduction in the personal level of hypocrisy, and the societies in which we live will be less burdened by hypocrisy as well. We have made the mistake, as a culture, of positing people as somehow different from their morality, a person/morality duality, and we have incorrectly surmised that because of the differences between our moral rhetoric and our moral actions we are separated from the responsibility to be our morality. We have made an excuse for our lack of moral constitution and have welcomed all too easily the shifting of the burden away from ourselves and toward a system full of human shortcoming. In truth, our morality is what we do and think and feel. The test of morality is whether we assume our responsibility and choose to live it and experience it as both mentality and action.

This is a critical point: people cannot be separate from their moral codes, for such action causes alienation and the destruction of self-confidence and security. This is exactly what Stephen Covey writes about in *The Seven Habits of Highly Effective People* when he discusses being morally centered. We must actually be our principles. To know oneself is to be moral, the source of one's own inner strength and conviction of belief, and to this end individual morality thus becomes a pillar, a source of strength and renewal in our drive to improve ourselves.

Now contrast this to the current situation, where very few individuals rely, as a source of their power, on their own morality. As a consequence of this, the "mission" of life, without a morality true to the individual, becomes nebulous and undirected as people are increasingly reluctant to rely on their own morality since they are not exactly sure what it is or if it should be different; the difference between what people believe their morality to be and what they actually do in their lives creates a type of alienation of the self. This alienation seeps into the entire being, creating an internal chaos that precludes development of a true moral order.

One of the goals of the new individualism must also be then to include the development of strategies whereby we can restructure our social institutions to promote reason so that the social conditioning process is one that supports individual moral responsibility and directs us toward internal moral initiative. As a society, we have generally failed to inculcate in our members a real belief in the self. Our entire national governing apparatus, through it's arrangement and certainly through it's action, delivers an inconsistency between what it stands for and what it does. This incongruence must be changed if we are to remedy the negative role that our institutions play within the moral development of our people.

With few exceptions, it is impossible to determine one's own morality without some kind of revelation, painful experience, or education; it is nearly impossible for even "enlightened" people to do so. To expect that our children can somehow manage this task without the proper training is fantasy. As a result, we must accept our role as parental liberators, safeguarding the rights of our children to make their own choices regarding morality after we have first demonstrated how it can be done by taking the difficult and trying steps ourselves. There can be no substitute for example. If we really want to change things, to improve ourselves and the world in which we live, not to mention safeguarding our children's futures, we must take decisive, personal action to make it happen; this is what the new individualism promises.

Morality, the New Individualism, and Change

We must remember, however, that true to our process framework, any sociological conditioning will be subject to challenge, even amendment, as individuals forever decide and determine what is moral. Sociologically, we have made the mistake that morality is somehow a constant, typical of our destination orientation, when a more constructive course would be to recognize that morality is itself a process and therefore subject to change over time. Moreover, moral constancy implies that morality is somehow pre-determined when in fact morality is forever mutable. It is only through our fear of the morally unknown that we cling to the morality of the past.

When we think of our current moral condition, we must accept that our cultural morality is essentially a legacy passed from generation to generation, certainly subject to some degree of change over time, but nevertheless formulated in times that contained significantly less complexity and were thus more or less stable. Is it logical to think that old moralities apply in today's world? Is it feasible to think that the morality of the past can somehow be sufficiently broad or capable of handling contemporary complexity? Do we really think that yesterday's morality can still be relevant?

It is impossible to categorize or predict every moral option. This fact alone invalidates the "pre-determination" or "time-tested" quality of current morality. In short, the basic premise behind current morality, that it is what it is because it is proven, is itself an illusion for it denies the changeability of morality over time and condition. Prior validity is not always an inexorable validity. The current system exalts the current morality over that of any disparate morality under the guise that the collective form is time-tested and thus applicable to all. If, however, we can proceed with the assumption that true morality must be an individual determination, then the imposition of any collective morality by definition compromises the individual, unless, of course, such a collective moral philosophy espouses, encourages, and guarantees complete moral freedom. The new individualism makes only one moral premise: that people are fully capable of their own moral construct.

The New Individualism as a Threat to Existing Morality

Fortunately, some people recognize that the current morality is fundamentally flawed and pursue a morality of their own. This takes tremendous courage, but without this step it is impossible to live a moral life. To some degree, these courageous individuals are truly pioneers, exploring truth and morality while often being labeled "flakes" and "crazys." This labeling is testament to the reinforcing, even self-correcting, nature of the collective moral conditioning of the people; challenges to the system are "put down" in order to perpetuate the existing moral code.

Before we get too angry at people within political parties or social institutions that are often only unwitting participants in this practice anyway, we need to remember that these actions are natural given our biological predisposition to fear and that people who oppose a change in morality genuinely feel threatened by any new code of conduct or moral standard. To facilitate an understanding of this, let's look at a quick example.

Even something as fortuitous as the end of the Cold War brings a societal reluctance to accept a new moral standard; since communism is no longer the enemy that it once was, what will replace it? What fills the moral gap between some foreign system and that of our own? If our morality has included a fight against communism, what will now be our moral fight? There is actually a dread among many people of life without a communist enemy simply because they will have to formulate and nurture a new morality, and this newness, really a fear of the unknown, terrifies people. Instead of moral opportunity these people feel moral abandonment.

The same dynamic occurs within our domestic perception of morality, for any change in the moral order is perceived to be a threat simply because we do not know what the new morality will be. An example of this is gays in the military which in and of itself, most studies conclude, has little effect on military capability or esprit de corps. But what the issue of gays in the military actually does is to threaten the current morality by challenging heterosexual moral domination and incorporating lifestyle alternatives that "menace" the prevailing sexual morality; this terrifies those who have prospered under the old moral framework.

Gays in the military is but one relatively small issue; imagine how threatening the new individualism will be to the existing moral order given the fact that people will undoubtedly choose moral codes that are better suited for themselves and will be correspondingly less concerned with preservation of the status quo. There can be little doubt that our moral futures will be substantially changed and that much control will be lost by those who seek the control of the moral order.

Moral Complacency

For most people, however, the existing morality is not intolerable; in fact, it often appears to work. But like so much else of familiarity, it works only because people are merely comfortable with the current system and have not been exposed to the alternative; if they have, they often lack the courage to try something new. Again, responsibility can be very difficult to accept and the possibility of constructing one's own morality can be so horrifying that for most people the choice is for no choice.

Moral complacency plays a large role in the lack of self-correction within our society; to a significant degree, our acceptance of the current moral standard encourages and perpetuates the status quo. In fact, our failure to consider moral alternatives carries a disproportionate influence relative to other factors because morality itself dominates a very large part of our cultural ethos. Morality is analogous to the "multiplier" effect in economics; its contribution goes way beyond what would appear to be its direct effect because it is so interrelated to everything else. This is why we must pursue moral alternatives since they carry disproportionate clout in any potential social restructuring.

Only exposure, through education, experience, or some as yet undeveloped method, can liberate individuals toward construction of their own true moral standards. Those who comprehend this dynamic and who truly understand the significance and possibilities inherent within a realistic approach to moral development have the burden of promoting the truth. Without their efforts, humanity will continue to believe in a morality of someone else's choosing and which runs counter to their own, true interests. We deserve to be morally free, with the responsibility and the reward that self-directed morality brings.

The Moral Tools of the New Individualism

To change our conception of morality requires a focus on methodologies that promise to deliver results and on approaches that also provide a framework of moral flexibility. Foremost among these is education, although not necessarily of the institutional variety. Since it is rather obvious that formalized educational approaches have failed to deliver the desired result, we must develop an educational motis operandi that is more fundamental; we must encourage more grass roots participation and less institutionalism within the educational process if we are to succeed.

People will readily respond to enhancements of their living experience if someone can demonstrate the benefits of such a change. This is especially true whenever the path can be shown to work through gradualism. Most people are fearful of sudden change and instead prefer a process whereby they can be "eased" into a transformation with minimal discomfort. The selling of the concept of a new morality must be done showing how people will benefit from it and also how a new morality can be gained using a gradualist approach.

The human psyche is keenly aware of things that improve the quality of life and we as people have a tendency to continue whatever it is that has made us feel better; this inherent drive will serve as a process reinforcer in the quest for an ever-improving morality. Once people acquire a taste for moral self-determination, a return to the previous morality will be less palatable; once we approve of our moving forward, it will be more difficult to go back.

In order for our moral educational effort to be successful, we must develop a process that provides human interface and interaction; most people require human association in order to feel comfortable and to increase their amenability to the process of change. This is exactly what is wrong with the existing textbook style approach, where written material substitutes for personal contact and where people are forced into a type of solitude that compromises the highly desirable interactive approach. Lastly, in a complex subject matter such as the construction of a moral code, humans respond much better to a human interpretation of moral history and theory than they do attempting to glean it from something as non-personal as text.

There is an experiential element as well which holds almost equal value to education, and it is ripe for cultivation by those committed to forwarding the true moral message: many people already feel that something is wrong, not only in their personal morality, but also in the morality of our culture. What they feel is the denial of the chance to construct a morality of their own choosing since so many moral choices are being made for them. People genuinely want to be in charge of their own lives, including their moral construct, because it feels good; it is only due to fear and disillusionment that we fail to assume our responsibility.

People, at least those sufficiently troubled, are beginning to demand a change of morality. Many also want more accurate and applicable codes of behavior and behavioral principles in which to direct their lives; moreover, some are insisting that cultural morality reflect these individual changes, almost as if they recognize, albeit unstrategically, that the whole must be changed to more favorably influence the parts. This, to a significant degree, explains that part within the social movement of multiculturalism that seeks a more inclusionary morality and a greater sense of equality through our shared humanity; if we can eliminate the exclusionary aspects of multiculturalism, the part that is ethnocentric to a fault, then humankind will have taken a dramatic step along the path of moral individualism.

The last tool of the new individualism in the implementation of a new morality is will; we have to want to force a change toward a more self-directed morality if we are to have any hope of making this dream a reality. Such a course requires an acceptance not only of our responsibility, but also of the seriousness and of the protracted nature of such an undertaking. Moreover, it also requires an understanding of the irreversibility of such action and mandates that moral progress must be won by people for people.

History, Morality, and Opportunity

If it is indeed true that history is carrying us toward a more individually driven moral future, then the existing moral order is imperiled. There can be no return to what once prevailed, no matter how intricate or collaborative the schemes to preserve the existing moral structure. The danger, however, lies with respect to the opportunity cost of time. Defenders of the status quo do possess the power to retard, with much undo suffering, the inevitable forward march of moral progression. This is similar to a general who, because of the superiority of his enemy, knows that he must ultimately surrender his city, but who for pride or ignorance resigns his compatriots to an unnecessary and tragic death.

If the new individualism is unleashed on society, the forces organized to preserve the status quo will fail to thwart its march as people increasingly begin to recognize the benefits of moral self-determination. As much as these defenders of the current system would like to believe, indeed prefer, that humanity is incapable of directing itself toward its own moral future, inevitably they will be forced to accede to numbers too large to overcome.

There are historical precedents to prove this is true, including the example of reason itself. In history, there were forces, primarily religious, who opposed the Age of Enlightenment and Reason because it fundamentally threatened their exalted positions. But what did their efforts gain them? As time passed, the reliance on human reason intensified, to the point where the abilities of the human intellect are now almost universally credited with the upward surge of humankind; any rational examination of human evolution clearly demonstrates the linkage between intellect and human progress, but because of knee-jerk resistance, enlightenment came later and with more travail than was necessary. Now, we are beginning to add intuition to reason and this will increase the pace of our moral self-determination if we can overcome the stigma of intuitive approaches.

We are presently at an unprecedented historical opportunity to formulate a new morality emphasizing freedom and the full extent of the human potential. It is no longer a debate of limits, but rather of what is possible. The forces of conservatism, who forever stress limitations as a guise for control, will inevitably be challenged to at least consider the desire to maximize the human potential. In the new individualism, the morality of self-degradation will shift to one of self-support, an attitude which bolsters further inquiries into the nature of our being and instills in us the confidence necessary to proceed even further into our own human cause. The new morality will not only be true, but perhaps for the first time, be rooted in truth.

This is not a minor point, for moralities have appeared to be true before. These earlier attempts at universal morality were, however, never founded on the most relevant moral precept, that being a morality that incorporates sufficiently developed "rational" codes of behavior based on adequate training as the moral prerequisite; never before did we include an emphasis on effective education and a self-supporting sociological conditioning process that would have enabled people to operate logically.

Those of us who recognize the responsibility of moral self-determination, as well as the rewards, grasp the force of history itself. Through this recognition, we contribute toward an increasingly moral future which we help shape and form. Whether we cause this new morality to occur with sweeping sociological impact in our time will ultimately be determined by the passion of our efforts. All that most of us require is a glimpse of that reality, through education or experience, to begin the process of introspection and moral self-determination that can liberate us all.

THE NEW INDIVIDUALISM

We, as humans, have an inner motivation to matter, to be significant, as we contribute toward the human condition in a meaningful and purposeful way.

There are few things we can do of more value than liberating others toward self-directed morality. The moral component of the new individualism is therefore one which strives to increase human freedom and self-determination because it is the most moral choice. Fundamentally, it is a belief in people and in their powers of reason, their wills, and their spirits. We must stop the moral arrogance of people who feel compelled to make our choices for us, and who, by doing so, deny us our freedom. We are not asking to become part of the existing moral order, but rather we are asking to formulate a morality of our own choosing by incorporating what is reasonable and rejecting what is illusory; moreover, we recognize that we are doing this for our own benefit and additionally for the fact that it can lead to much related progress for the entire human family. And, as we shall soon see, we know that this also makes us powerful.

7

Power

We have already discussed, at least peripherally, the concept of power; until now, however, we have focused primarily on the relative power of people versus society or what we might call external or non-personal power versus that of the individual. Moreover, we have also identified that morality is closely linked to power and so we must also examine the implications of what the quest for self-determined morality means for the development of personal power.

The concept of individual power is probably more correctly called empowerment, and certainly there is much to be learned about society from the study of individual power, for societies are often "empowered" in the same way as are society's members. The concept of empowerment, of being made more powerful than before, is really an extension of our evolutionary progression and dovetails with our innate desire to extend our capabilities. As a result, we need to understand what empowerment will mean for people and their cultures since empowerment promises to fundamentally alter the structure of society. Structural change is never an isolated event for invariably it has an effect on everything which follows it, and for this reason individual empowerment can produce a systemic change that may in fact cause subsequent generations to live more powerfully as they become increasingly aware of their own, expanding power.

We must also examine the concept of power within the framework of increasing technological sophistication; in short, how will individual empowerment fit within a rapidly expanding and sophisticated technological world. This is nothing more than a call for developing a method for managing technological change before it manages us; in fact, this might be the most urgent concern that we as a people have. First, however, we must examine what has transpired historically with respect to power, both individually and collectively.

Individual and Collective Power

In the past, most people have not felt empowered; as a result, virtually all the power has resided in some ambiguous "external" whose actions and dictums formed the bulk of the socialization process and contributed inexorably toward the powerlessness of the average human being. Occasionally, however, there were glimpses of the power potential of people, such as that occurred in the French Revolution, the American Revolution, and the various national liberation movements that have occurred throughout the twentieth century; these movements rejected the existing power paradigms and were largely attempts by people to take control of their own lives, albeit through a leadership not always completely altruistic or wholly aligned with the interests of the people they purportedly represented; at least, however, the new leadership generally proclaimed the same basic motivations as that of the people and so we can count these examples as the closest thing possible to a true "people" movement.

Although individual power has no doubt increased because power elite transitions have occurred more frequently and have therefore had less time and opportunity to become more firmly entrenched or more institutionalized, humanity nevertheless finds itself without any real aggregate self-power. In short, although power elites have been forced to become more representative of the people in order to preserve their own power, a prime example being the case of Chile and general Pinochet, humanity is still insufficiently empowered relative to its potential or what is necessary for true self-determination.

We have never really experienced self-government; our form of government, representative democracy, is largely an elitist system and has thus proven woefully inadequate contrasted to the collective needs of our people. Although the best system yet devised, it is clearly in need of a major change. As technological progression accelerates at almost unimaginable rates, we must develop a "people power" system in order to manage our future. The concept of top-down government or other elitist structures, which through their design shortrift real participatory democracy, will simply work no longer. We must shift the power to people and direct power internally if we are to handle the large scale requirements for the survival of our species; everyone must participate and be responsible if we are to succeed since elites can no longer manage, unilaterally or multilaterally, the sum of the world's affairs. In the current global situation, we are facing a problem of enormous complexity which can only be superintended if everyone acts in a responsible way; the scope of the global problem is beyond any elite's ability to effectively deal with it and the prospects of an elitist improvement in the future are decreasing by the hour.

The Goal of Individual Power

As we have seen, an individually empowered life fundamentally means freedom, choice, and complete responsibility for one's own actions and thought processes; it also means respect of the same framework for others. Most importantly, it suggests a mental state sufficiently advanced to recognize the damage to ourselves and to our society through an external directedness. We have discussed the importance of constructing a mental model capable of rejecting any collective morality that is lacking in rational foundation, and we have also seen that this mental model assumes an ever-evolving and advancing logical decision-making process capable of recognizing the process orientation that is "natural" or inherently "self-evident" within the evolutionary dynamic; moreover, through this we also further recognize our individual ability and necessity to positively influence the future course of humanity.

Furthermore, we have seen that such a mental model also suggests a paradigm where people will have the power, essentially the confidence, to trust their own sense of judgement and select the life path which they inherently know is best for them. We all possess this internal cognizance, although most of us are not currently connected to it.

Individual empowerment also means accomplishment to a level commensurate with what is best for us, without pressure or obligation to fulfill any agendas other than our own. Again, we all possess an internal understanding, once we become connected to ourselves, that allows us to know the level of success that balances our need for achievement with our other interests and motivations. Naturally, the levels of accomplishment among individuals will be as unique and singular as we are. Gone will be the expectation of striving to achieve levels that others have determined for themselves, and assumed for us, simply because these expectations will be irrelevant; such an understanding invariably means less insecurity for we will no longer feel compelled to measure up to any standard other than our own.

This tendency to "keep up" with others is one of the most burdensome and destructive tendencies in the whole of human experience for it has helped to fuel the perception of individual inadequacy; although certainly a by-product of evolutionary competition, this tendency has failed to recognize the qualitative differences in people and how each can contribute toward the "good of the species" through the advancement of their own personal power. The converse of this, the interests of the species being "forwarded" by an elitist power structure, works only if that elite is leading the species in a direction that is advantageous for all. To a large extent, we have placed our personal futures on "equidistancing" relative to the position of those in power on the assumption that they could best safeguard our interests as we rode the coattails of their progression. But what if this base assumption is wrong? What if our elites are nothing more than lemmings leading us off a cliff?

So what does the goal of individual power look and feel like if the power of an "external" is inadequate? Individual empowerment necessarily means a stronger sense of self and a diminishment of fear and insecurity. It implies a greater ability to be introspective, yet it also infers a greater willingness to form better business and social relationships because such introspection makes us more valuable to others. As they gain from our new, improved versions of ourselves so we will gain from our effect on them. Frankly, they will have more to offer and so will we. Moreover, the wholeness of the individual will be the chief criteria for whether we are successful and we will shift from a zero/sum worldview to one that emphasizes mutual benefit as the most productive avenue toward real self-interest.

We will know that we can best prosper through mutual respect and trust, that it is self-interested to support others in their personal quest for self; most importantly, we will know that these mutual benefits can come only through the execution of our responsibility toward ourselves and toward a system which first seeks the establishment of an environment where our new individualism can flourish. We will know that to control is to choke, that we can never receive what we require from others if we do not in turn grant them the freedom they need to make their own choices. We must trust in their abilities and we must let them choose to trust and respect us.

To do this, we first need to trust ourselves so that we can have the personal security to be patient and understanding if they do not choose our course. We must be secure in ourselves, to the point that we are capable of handling unfavorable choices made by others in the exercise of their freedom. Again, the process toward individual empowerment is a long one, but we know that through confidence we can develop the perseverance necessary to achieve our goal.

Individual Power and Personal Fear

The positive implications of individual empowerment are too enormous to be discussed it totality; many could not even be contemplated yet. But one of the most rewarding would be the elimination of fear, which has been and continues to be the scourge of our species and the single greatest factor in the denial of our full potential. The elimination of fear, particularly the fear of death and the capitulation of our responsibility to others through teleology, would do more to access people's capabilities than any other course we could choose.

To reject teleology and to use our personal responsibility as motivation to maximize our time here on earth is the definition of empowerment. Within this acceptance lies the potential to eliminate counterproductive and suppressive external directedness and the opportunity to seize personal choice as our vehicle of liberation. Freedom of choice grounded in reason, which is really the meaning of self-determination, is the very device whose recognition provides the liberation necessary to transform power from someone else to ourselves.

Those who have exercised choice for us have made a joke of democracy. Do we really want to condemn future generations to more of the same, to a governmental structure which becomes increasingly subject to special interest, bureaucracy, and inattentiveness to our concerns? Do we really want to let others choose our political and socio-economic futures? Do we want to proceed on a course which guarantees only our inevitable decline?

Do we want to continue to be afraid of the alternative of external rule, of personal power?

Because of our insecurity, we have allowed others to assume power even when confronted with the knowledge of their ineptitude. Look at our own national experience: not long ago, we had tremendous faith in government and the business community, and we trusted this alliance to lead us. And throughout history, there has been an obvious tendency toward authoritarianism or power elitism that resulted from the belief, even among the enlightened few, that people were best served through a national interest embodied in the political-economic structure of the country. Plato's *Republic* is a prime example, as was the Roman tendency toward increased concentrations of power in the furtherance of national interest. Even today, we admire and seek to emulate the Japanese example of state and business amalgamation. But we have seen, especially in the Roman example, that irreverence for the people ultimately collapses the system; invariably, only people can rule themselves because the enormity of the task demands full participation. The lack of real participatory involvement, that is, all people being fully committed to their own futures and made capable through proper training and rational foundation, is the reason why all civilizations inevitably collapse; until we overcome our fear and rule ourselves, we will end up exactly like those societies that preceded us.

The perpetuation of human insecurity is perhaps the ultimate tragedy in the history of humankind, for the full potential of the human being has been compromised as a result. Think of the lives that could have been and never were because people were afraid to harvest their power. Think of the wasting of life juxtaposed to the opportunity that empowered living brings. Contemplate the discoveries that could have been but that never were simply because people could not break through their fear; all of this is so sad and so horrible in its consequence that it seems that heretofore the human experience has been little more than an attempt to faintly glimpse what might be. The sum of the great undertakings in human history, our building of societies, the creation of language, our technological progression and our scientific explorations are all but a tip of the proverbial iceberg. We have no idea what can be accomplished if we increase our power through the elimination of our fear and dedicate ourselves toward the expansion of our capabilities.

Personal Power and the Contemporary World

In the world of today, it is becoming increasingly evident that some incredible changes are underway in the nature of the human experience; the proliferation of information, the condensation of human society (global village), the computer age, and the spiritual exploration of the self all signal dramatic changes in the way we relate to each other. Certainly, whatever transformations are taking place will be characterized by great strife as the old gives way to the new; much of our contemporary experience is really this story. The movement toward a new beginning is also really about human liberation, about finding ourselves, and about the urgency of managing our futures given the speed of change.

In America, we have heralded this global movement toward freedom in typically narrow and exclusive terms, as a triumph of capitalism over communism or democracy over totalitarianism; this is far too simplistic. In actuality, the movement we are witnessing is a further evolution toward individual power and self-determination and is not simply a case of a triumphant economic or political system. What has not been discussed, at least what our leadership and our news media have failed to notice, is that the global movement toward human liberation is a fundamental evolutionary progression central to the survival of the species.

Even within our own country, we are witnessing a citizenry so disaffected with the status quo that we have demanded a change in the nature of power and called for a significant reduction in the old power elite structure; the Clinton election is a good example of people opting for a try at something new; we are demanding greater access and we are getting it. As citizens, we are also insisting on more self-determination and more individual responsibility, and we are voting in politicians who use their power to increase the powers of individuals. We are attempting to move away from a political and economic system that safeguards the interests of the few and we are instead seeking one that is more in touch with the people who give it power.

With the intensity of the Information Age propelling the world into unchartered territory at an alarming rate, we must include all people in the directional course of our species; this is where our current efforts at change fall short, for they lack a truly inclusionary nature for all. We must realize the inexorable relationship between personal power and successful management of the world's affairs. Why is this so? Because the intensity of the forces unleashed in the modern world carries with it unprecedented magnitude and consequence for the human family. The stakes are simply too high not to include all of our people. We will need everyone on the same page in order for us to do our required reading and ensure that through this reading we give subsequent generations the chance to read better than we have. Fear dies a slow and protracted death, and the power that has resulted from the manipulation of that fear fights with everything in its being to preserve itself. The movement toward a new individualism is a high stakes game, one that fundamentally challenges and seeks to overthrow a system which frequently has run counter to the human interest, and is therefore more of a quest for the soul of humankind than it is a political or economic cause. The new individualism is much more base, more binary, as simple as black and white or good and bad. We all need to be advised that the old ways die hard and that the fight will be as intense, painful, and horrific as any fight we have ever undertaken; most importantly, we must realize that the contemporary setting ensures that this fight will happen. The world's complexity and corresponding challenges are actually forcing us to choose, and the choice will be one which we must make for ourselves to advance ourselves.

The End of Teleology

If we can promote individual responsibility of the kind that ultimately leads to individual empowerment, then we will come to know that our choices determine national policies, global events, and the course of the world's direction. Once we know this, we will know that events are not predetermined and that the present must be managed so that the future can be enjoyed. Critics might respond that this is self-evident. But is it? If it were, would we be destroying our planet and would we still possess a cultural worldview that is almost unbelievably short-term oriented and thus so shortsighted? We, as a people, have been afraid to accept this social responsibility for the same reason that individuals choose to live the choices that others have made for them: to avoid responsibility and accountability for outcomes because of a fear that we may make a wrong choice or otherwise prove our incompetence. But we can no longer afford to be insecure.

Almost overwhelmingly, the most significant recognition that we can make is the one disposing of teleology. To accept that there is nothing meant to happen and that therefore we determine our own futures is to accept that individual responsibility is the only way to become truly powerful; this is the definition of personal power. What has transpired in the human past and what will transpire in the human future will be the result of human choice. What we can be sure of is that more rational and less fearful choices will result if we choose to take this course; we also know that we will be happier since happiness is best achieved when people are in charge of their own destinies and making logical decisions regarding their lives and the course of their society.

Human Progress, Power, and Technology

The future appears bright if we can get there. Using an historical perspective, it is clearly evident that the forward progression of human development has, as a by-product of that development, produced almost overwhelming technological change. It would almost appear that human development is now the story of managing technology, and some would suggest that our lack of successful management techniques imperil our humanity since we are not managing very well. Moreover, there is reason to believe that most people, even our technological managers, underestimate the enormity and importance of this task; it remains, however, a task inherent in our existence and one which we must master.

Some would argue that in the future, those who control technology will be the powerful; in the current interpretation of power, this is probably true. It is much more advantageous, however, to conceptualize technology not as a means for a furtherance of power, but rather as a tool of empowerment. Technology will provide its maximum benefit when it is utilized to assist the development of the human potential, as opposed to maintaining technology in its current role as primarily one of economic support or advance. Today, technology is viewed as a helper to humankind within an existing framework of economic and social development that decries technology as more than that, including technology as a liberator of the human spirit; unfortunately, this framework contains all of the individually limiting aspects discussed throughout this book and therefore current technology cannot be used to liberate the human potential to its fullest extent as long as the mission of technology remains unchanged.

The advocacy for the development of technological advancement that more completely benefits the human potential need not be threatening since it does not jeopardize our fundamental humanity, but rather improves upon it. Moreover, such a technological focus, being one designed to liberate our capabilities, will carry a tremendous economic benefit as well; technology should not be used merely to "speed up" productivity, but rather to unleash it. Technology can greatly accelerate the journey into the full extension of the human potential if we choose to let it.

Presently, there are many who express a general fearfulness regarding a furthering of technological progression based on the perception that humanity cannot maintain comprehensive pace with the full extent of technological advancement; because technology proceeds faster that people can adapt to it, the belief is that technology is out of control. This exacerbates the feeling that the future is already "getting away from us." This is a natural fear. Moreover, it is an indictment of the current inability to manage technological change. The "gap" that exists between those with technological abilities, what is essentially understanding and developing technologies, and those without is widening and there does not appear to be a self-correcting mechanism whereby humanity can gain control over our technological future. The net result is that our inability to manage technological progression is actually increasing the level of fear instead of eliminating it. If we can change the course of technology to further human needs, we can incorporate these people into our mutual technological future.

As proof that this fear is real, consider that many of our most deeply felt social horrors, expressed in literature and cinema, have centered on technological advancement: Orwell's Big Brother having the full disposal of technology to control populations, Huxley's drug of the future reducing humankind to little more than functionaries, and an assortment of terminators, robots, and cyborgs forever challenging humankind for dominance and control of the planet, all demonstrate the fear of what technology might mean for the human condition.

Although it is doubtful that technology itself, through its own intellect, poses a threat to humankind it may indirectly do so through the misguided efforts of people who seek technology as a useful tool of social control. This is especially true of certain governments, Saddam Hussein's Iraq for example, and probably true of certain businesses or industries as well. The latter cases are perhaps most threatening of all since they are not readily identifiable enemies to be vanquished, but are in fact protected and encouraged through our current management of technology.

Clearly, this is not science fiction; an excellent case can be made that we are destroying the planet through improper and destructive use of technology, especially that of economic production and consumption, and there appears to be very little, if any, effective management of the problem. The motivations behind this environmental destruction are largely monetary, although there are other reasons as well. But, in the final analysis, it is not technology that is at fault, but our inability to use it effectively and for the right purposes.

One example of misguided "technothought" is the pursuit of technology for technology's sake. We have a built-in preference for technological progress, even when it is unmanaged, because of the fundamental assumption that all technological progression is a testament to the human mind and therefore must be forwarded; when technology is added to capitalism, what forms is an almost inexorable link between technology and economic progression without due consideration for the environmental and human costs. This is exacerbated in the belief that anything aligned with capitalistic advance must be in the human interest as well. Now firmly established through our Cold War victory, this link is extremely difficult to sever and represents a huge obstacle in the quest for personal power. This is an extremely significant sociological concern, and one that the new individualism must address if people are to proceed toward their full potential.

To manage this technological advancement will require a Herculean effort since technological advancement is proceeding at a rate faster than current forms of management can successfully control, and far too few people realize it; the net result of this is a a subculture demanding technological "reform." Some of this reform is embodied in the environmental movement and some in the increasingly popular questioning of globalism, space exploration and economic production processes. Further signs of this reform movement are the return to certain religious practices, stress management techniques and personal growth seminars designed to provide relief from the effects of technology. Even Naisbitt's "high touch" is an example of what might be called "coping strategies" to deal with technological advance.

Technology and the New Individualism

The failure within society to effectively manage technological change leaves only one viable option: individual responsibility. The future of human survival will be forever linked with the ability to individually manage technological change while simultaneously preserving our essential individual freedom and self-determination; in short, we must not become "technohumans" who are more influenced by technology than vice versa. We must learn to manage the rate of change, concomitant with the ability of humankind to preserve our freedom if we are to progress further into the human potential; if we fail to do this, we will become slaves to technology, unfocused and without a direct mission for what technological advancement can mean for us.

The external directedness inherent in our culture which we have discussed throughout has important implications for the management of technology; essentially we have had what amounts to the control of technology by the few, and to this extent, technology has been used for the purposes of perpetuating the status quo and for maintaining existing power. More damaging still, technology has been intertwined with economic performance, the vanguard of the elite, and although this has not necessarily been the only culprit, it has certainly occurred with substantial opportunity cost.

We have made the same mistake with technology that we have made with our economic philosophy, that growth is the indisputable goal, and we have never really considered the full costs involved in such an mindset. We have been almost entirely focused on growth, to the point that increasing Gross Domestic Product through technological exploitation is considered a national priority regardless of the environmental or human costs. Technology has indeed comprised a huge part of our Gross Domestic Product, so it is easy to understand how we have equated technology with our continued economic prosperity. Our economic philosophy has been our directive, even our imperative, and we have sought the implementation and utilization of technology in pursuit of that objective in a way that disregards virtually any countervailing views.

The task of technological management that faces the new individualism is enormous. Why? Because technology tends to perpetuate the existing power structure since, like growth economics, it becomes extremely difficult to stop or reverse course. As a rule, the more advanced the technological state the more difficult becomes the challenge of identifying its original purpose and changing its direction; the further away becomes the original purpose, the more purposeless becomes the technology. We have already seen this evidenced in our time: the destruction of the environment, the meaningless development of absolutely absurd weapons systems, health care inefficiencies caused by over-utilization of technology as compared to holistic, preventative medicine, and even the utilization of entertainment alternatives (Multimedia, the new human "liberator?") that serves as a substitute for proper parenting. These examples show that the original purpose of technology, to assist human effort, may in fact be leading us toward our own demise.

Clearly, to question the purpose of technology, to demand an evaluation of it, is to question the ability of our external-directedness framework to manage our technological futures. For the political and cultural elites who have been the beneficiaries of this framework an evaluation of technology is threatening. When we question the purpose and management of technology, we also demand accountability; people in privileged positions despise accountability, for only accountability can cause a reevaluation of their status. As a result, they tend to avoid discussion or debate regarding their performance and the technology which supports them.

Often this concern manifests itself in a zero/sum game where technological failures are not readily admitted for fear that their exposure will cause a reevaluation of those entrusted with its course; technologies failing to reach their stated objectives are condoned through pronouncements that attempt to exonerate the original purpose through the explanation that periodic failures are necessary for future development. Such was the case with the Strategic Defense Initiative, in that it was funded and justified while the enemy for which it was intended crumbled in front of us; this is not just a case of misguided policy, but also of technology misdirected.

We have examined what empowerment means and how our future empowerment must necessarily entail control over technology for the purpose of improving our lives. But the concept of empowerment, individual power, is akin to so many of the other concepts discussed in this book that it must be seen as an interconnection, as opposed to an extension. Empowerment does not result from the functions of the other aspects of our lives, but rather is the synergistic consequence of our self-directedness in all areas, including the control over technology. The more purposefully directed we live, the clearer becomes the direction of technology and our sense of power over it. When we know more of our potential, we will know more of what to do with technology.

To be powerful necessitates controlling our environment and this is why the management of technology is so crucial. We have reached that point in the evolutionary process whereby we may not be sufficiently intelligent to guarantee the sustenance of the planet, but we are sufficiently intelligent to destroy it. We have developed technologies that are capable of wholesale destruction and can obliterate life as we know it and yet we proceed down paths which daily threaten our species and our home. We have put a blind faith in technology instead of a trust in ourselves. We are only now beginning to understand the extent of our power, and hopefully this simple vision will be ample motivation for us to change course and guarantee for ourselves a more benevolent future.

8
Synthesis

Throughout this book, there has been a central theme of people attempting to find their potential through a maze of complexity, illusion, insecurity, and lack of sociological promise. We have seen that there has historically been much to overcome if we are to change into more of what we want to be. In addition, we have seen that our continuing evolution is a collective matter as well as an individual one and that whatever principles or direction emerges from our self-inquiry must apply to all people. Within this framework, this book can be viewed correctly as anti-elitist, people-oriented, and self-directed.

People, Not Politics

Although the intention has not been for this book to be a political work per se, there are certainly many political overtones discussed throughout. Interestingly, the book is an espousal of neither conservative nor liberal ideology; to be sure, there are many "conservative" positions taken, such as a reliance on individuals and a reverence for America, but there are also some "liberal" postulates as well, such as the challenging of religion, an honest evaluation of our political heritage, and a criticism of the traditional family. Moreover, although both conservatives and liberals ardently defend capitalism and differ really only about the management or lack of management of the economy, this book has called into question much of the "sacredness" of our economic system, specifically that of "growth economics" that do not always serve the interests of people. Given this, we have seen here that people predominate over political/economic concerns because people are most important.

If this book has been too political at times, it is really a function of a general predisposition by it's subject matter to be politically deterministic; anytime socio-economic issues are discussed, invariably they become political. Even an issue as base as human happiness and how to construct it is a political issue. We know that there is a fundamental interconnectedness between human drives and political discourses, and so the book has been arranged to flow from individuals to society since people and their political structures must always interact, connect, and form.

In any event, the book contains many sociological, political, economic, philosophical, biological, historical, and cultural elements although it is really a book about people and how to improve ourselves. Even though a large sociological benefit will result, the "story" here is really about us, individual lives that deserve to be lived at the highest order. We must never lose sight of this fact; it is very easy to get lost in the macro focus and as a result fail to see each human benefit. If this book has erred, it is probably by not providing a better "picture" of what each individual life can become through an acceptance of the new individualism, although perhaps it is better for each reader to speculate and dream about how their lives can improve. After all, the vision of each life should belong to that life, for it is that life that ultimately forms that vision.

Synthesis

The purpose of this chapter, then, will be to integrate and synthesize what has been discussed thus far and mold it into some comprehensive whole; moreover, we will also identify the full extent of the opposition and clarify what must be done to overcome it.

As a society, we seem to be on the verge of a mental paradigm shift toward a synthesis of knowledge and away from exclusionary specialization; as Thomas Kuhn noted in *The Structure of Scientific Revolutions,* whenever an old paradigm becomes incapable of explaining the current situation a new paradigm displaces it. Moreover, the new paradigm merely has to explain more than the old or competing ones, not all of the facts of the new circumstance. As a result, our new paradigm appears to be one which offers increased choice and viable alternatives as opposed to pervasive indecision and inherent limitations since the old paradigm of "limited options" cannot satisfactorily manage our contemporary setting.

The general benefits of this framework have been discussed here, but it is also possible to follow the specifics in our daily lives. So much of the new paradigm is already evident, revealed in our daily media with reports of progress in such fields as management, education, medicine, philosophy, astronomy, and many other areas of study, and because of this we can take confidence that at least the potential for our potential is there. These are exciting times, with the combinative benefits of such a synthetic approach extremely encouraging.

In this chapter, we will specifically discuss something which is very difficult to define but which also is a very real threat to our futures: system inertia. This is the whole of the opposition referred to earlier in this chapter. When we look at the current state of the world, particularly that of America, we see evidence that we are being victimized by an inertia that stifles constructive change and which ominously predisposes us toward a general sociological deterioration. This is why much of the book has examined complacency and apathy because until we recognize the full extent of the problem, we are powerless to do anything about it.

Before we can examine system inertia and how the new individualism might serve to mitigate it, we must first review some of the "fundamentals" discussed in the previous chapters and combine them into a framework that more clearly focuses in our intent.

The Framework of the Future

The most fundamental of our sociological needs is the creation of a self-corrective mechanism whereby society can change itself from what appears to be a self-destructive course. The lack of a self-corrective mechanism is at the root of our incongruity with our society. We know, all of us, that we are perilously close to an irreversible decline of our culture and that we must right our ship. Americans feel this disharmony and we know that we must understand where the mistakes have been made so that we can improve upon our futures.

We have longed for a self-correction not of our own making and we have wished that somehow, almost magically, the system of which we are such an inescapable part might cure itself without our help. We are afraid of how much effort we will truly have to make, and if such an effort is to be the result of our own self-responsibility, then we begin to naturally doubt our abilities and our staying power for the task at hand.

The shifting of responsibility away from others and to ourselves is absolutely terrifying since to be successful we must confront our own inadequacies. We must see what we do not want to see and become what we do not think we can become. The challenge is enormous, for it entails a journey into ourselves, where we are afraid and insecure and vulnerable. We must look deep within, into the realm of the possible, and we know that one of the possibilities is failure. We are afraid to confront the reality that we might fail, and so we close our eyes in denial of the travail that we find ourselves in. But on some level, deep inside us, we know that we must eventually fight this fight.

Moreover, we know that the vast majority of us live in a fearful state and that we think defense before we think opportunity. But we also know that the solutions to our problems lie in eliminating fear for everyone, since anyone who lives in fear causes a reciprocal fear in others. If we are going to share, all of us, in the vision of opportunity and individual capability, then we must first reduce and then eliminate fear or the vision will not form. This task seems awesome, even beyond our capabilities, but surely it is not and we must get there and make the vision a reality.

Given that, let's take a look through some logical sequencing at what forms the foundation for the new individualism and its vision for the future.

The new individualism is a by-product of the following logic:

> People are the ultimate power and the greatest hope for their future…
>
> Through our natural fear-based worldview, however, we have failed to assume our power and have languished instead in an externally-directed state…
>
> Because fear-basing is so intrinsic and pervasive, we must utilize a systemic approach in combating it…
>
> And we must study history to see how the past has contributed to who we are today…
>
> Moreover, history clearly shows that existence is process oriented…
>
> And that the dynamic of evolutionary progression, itself a process, is fundamental to human existence…
>
> As a result of our evolutionary drive, we have developed societies where the socialization process becomes paramount in the advance of our species…
>
> And given this recognition, we live in extremely opportunistic times since through this acknowledgment we have the possibility of changing the socialization process to our advantage…

By emphasizing responsibility and choice, combined with reason and intuition…

We can develop understanding to eliminate the illusion and hypocrisy inherent in our system, and through proper parenting we can break the cycle of illusion perpetuation and change the socialization process itself…

We feel the added impetus to undertake this task because the twin threats of unmanaged globalism and technological progression greatly imperil ourselves and our planet…

And by meeting this threat and succeeding, we can improve the quality of life for ourselves and safeguard the futures of our children…

To be successful, however, we must develop new strategies, and we must end the singular reliance on education to inculcate in people self-responsibility and self-power. We must find ways to stop the onslaught of our shortsightedness.

Managing an Unreasonable Advance

As humankind "progresses" toward a globalism and a technological explosion whose primary by-product is increasing complexity, we must begin to understand the danger associated in a world that begins to take on more of the self-destructive characteristics of those societies causing the greatest intensification of the problem: the industrialized and advanced "North." The more complexity that exists, the more the status quo and its self-destructive path is facilitated since it becomes even less likely in the future to be able to discern what is wrong; complexity masks system inadequacies, becoming a fog that obscures the need to change.

A simple example from business will illustrate the point: International Business Machines, whose tremendous size, myriad connections, product lines, and personnel layers camouflaged a fundamental flaw in their organization. IBM could not progress because the complexities of the techno-business environment had transcended their ability to understand them. Certainly, hubris had something to do with their troubles, but the trends that escaped IBM's management group were not as self-evident as some revisionists would have us believe, and arrogance alone cannot explain their dilemma. IBM's primary flaw was an unmanageable complexity that manifested itself as system inertia, which was also essentially indiscernible to those who ran IBM. By becoming so complex, IBM lacked the ability to foresee necessary changes and consequently they were unable to make revisions until a financial crisis had ensued.

Any system, whether it be a corporation, government, or society is subject to the same laws as that of IBM. In fact, larger systems like a society are even more vulnerable because they are even tougher to change or reposition. For this reason, we must be concerned about our nation. Most of our leaders, although recognizing "gridlock," fail to understand the truly systemic nature of the problem. Because these individuals have a vested interest in the status quo, they either cannot or do not want to see how increasing complexity threatens the continuation of the system they so desperately seek to hold.

We can look to the economic philosophy of Joseph Schumpeter and his concept of economic change through destructive economic processes to prove this point. Schumpeter believed that destruction of a system leads to a more constructive replacement, and although he was referring to an economic dynamic, we can extrapolate his framework of change up to the sociological level. It may well be in fact that large portions of our social system will simply fade away or collapse, and that society as we know it today will change in many new and drastic ways; it is fully possible that what exists today will be replaced by a more functional system, at least we should all hope so. After all, contemporary society is barely recognizable from where it was even fifty years ago. It is, however, just as likely that the replacement system could be more destructive, such as what occurred with the collapse of the Weimar Republic that gave rise to Hitler and nazism or the collapse of the Kerensky Government that led to the Bolshevik Revolution and communism. For this reason, we must do everything within our power to ensure that the replacement system is effective and enduring and that it possesses first and foremost the interests of people.

The point here is simple: change must be managed, anticipated proactively in order to develop a new system that ensures the perpetuation of an order committed to improving the human condition; this effort must be directed, focused, and planned. If we do not purposefully direct this effort, we will continue in an ad hoc manner which can only mean an intensification of the misdirected course of our futures. This is the hope of the new individualism, to change the aimless momentum so characteristic of our current sociological condition.

Lastly, we must clearly seek to understand the relationship between an emerging and intensifying globalism and the increasing complexity that it causes; since we have not managed, at least effectively, the complexity that occurs in a single society, how can we be expected to handle the additional load that globalism will inevitably cause? Most of the press devoted to the concept of globalism is favorable, i.e., that it offers the greatest hope for world peace or for working together to solve world problems, but is this really a likely scenario? Isn't it just as likely that globalism will accelerate the degree of complexity and its corresponding unmanageability? What makes us think that we can rise to the occasion when we have not been able to do so in simpler times? Do we think that more intricate and expanding problems will increase our ability to control them? Do we really think that a command system that seeks to micromanage the world's affairs through the United Nations or other global organizations will work? Do we want our world to be managed through a global elite, even potentially more powerful than our national one?

Globalism and the exacerbation of a more complex and unmanageable worldwide situation is an already scary phenomenon and an even more frightening prospect. The joining of the world to more of the world, which increases the mass and the magnitude of the sum, is hopeful only if the aggregate promises to be an improvement on its predecessor. If the direction of the mass is to increase its own destructive possibilities in an even more destructive way, what have we gained by causing this mass? An increased likelihood of our own survival or extinction?

Clearly, we have unleashed forces which threaten our very existence; nuclear weapons, pollution, and overpopulation are very real threats. Because we have not killed ourselves yet does not mean that we will not. We may simply be proceeding down the path toward that end, rather oblivious to what we have wrought with our ignorance. Like the child who continues to eat candy until he/she is sick, we cannot seem to stop ourselves. As a result, we must do whatever is in our power to make sure that we eat only that which we can handle, and no more. Moreover, we must question the system that allowed the child access to so much candy in the first place, in order to guard against that part of ourselves that unreasonably proceeds toward our own demise. Since it may be unrealistic to expect the child to do so on his/her own, we must create a system whereby the child is protected until that time when his/her reason guarantees his/her own comfort. If the system does not allow for such a protection, we must form a system that does.

System Inertia

In preceding chapters, there is an obvious criticism of the current system. We have discussed at length the absence of a self-correcting mechanism and the corresponding continuation of a flawed sociological structure that imperils our very survival. We have also discussed how this state is largely unrecognized, preserved through a reverence for what has preceded us in time and a respect for what currently exists. Yet all of us know and feel that something is wrong and that "it" needs fixing. But we also know that what we must fight is a beast, a monster, incredibly powerful and strong and seemingly invincible. Yet for all of its size, the monster is evasive, difficult to engage or to even see, and this complicates the strategies to be deployed against it.

The monster to which we are referring is system inertia, that firmly entrenched and foreboding mass whose staying power has thus far proved resistant to efforts designed to overcome it. System inertia is a particularly evil enemy, for through its very existence it saps the life right out of those who seek to destroy it; in many ways, it is analogous to an HIV virus that gradually weakens our bodies and our spirits until we are eventually overcome by our inability to fight on. The components of system inertia, such as fear, illusion, hypocrisy, ineptitude, unreasonableness, and ignorance finally weaken us like so many opportunistic infections and we succumb through resignation. We give up because there is no cure in sight and so we lose hope and resolve.

System inertia strikes at the core, at our political, economic, and social structures and at our relations with people. Virtually every institution and every social interaction is plagued with inertia, the weight of an immobile and bloating jumble that stifles our good intentions to live more productively. It is the root of frustration and procrastination, for through the perceived inability to forcibly extract it, we shrink to sloth, compliance, and disinterest.

System Inertia and Us

System inertia is a cultural, even global problem, but it begins with people. The full spectrum of human interaction is fundamentally characterized by a general frustration in our relations with people, usually because we know that we want more than we are getting from our relationships and from our institutions. We must see that until people, individuals and the groups that they form, confront this inertia on an individual basis, we cannot hope to change the world and make it what we want it to be. System inertia is much more than that part of a larger system of dysfunction, it is also a much smaller part that starts with every single person. It is that part of us that lags behind our dreams and that fails to bridge the gap between who we are and what we are capable of.

System inertia is what we hate about our world; it is war, poverty, hunger, deterioration, racism, sexism, devaluation, and irresolution. It is that part of us that does not want enough, that does not have the will to succeed. It is the tragedy of living without really living, of roles and places and what others want. It is the elimination of meaning and the loss of purpose, the fading of light and the imprisonment of darkness, and it is that side of ourselves that we do not wish to see but that are reminded of daily.

If our political and economic system is in jeopardy and our cultural and moral collapse a real possibility, it is because we have failed to understand our enemy and see it for what it is. But this is a totally different type of enemy, for only this enemy contains within its being the seeds of our own salvation. It is an enemy who must be saved, an enemy who must be defeated but not killed. We must turn this enemy like a foreign spy, one that we convince should work for us because there is more personal benefit in doing so. We must understand that system inertia is us, and we must also understand that only we have the power to transform this inertia into a friend simply by changing our view of it. The intricate connections of human relation can be used in furtherance of a social benefit if we will first see the dream.

We must move away from zero/sumism and compromise and instead move toward a framework of win/win. Nothing is more fundamental for our success than this restructured dynamic since through it we can control our fear and move on to accept new ideas. The restructuring of our mental model from zero/sum to win/win is a grandiose idea, one full of promise and aspiration, but also one denigrated by those locked into exclusionary worldviews. If we do not embrace amenability to new ideas, we cannot mentally restructure and we cannot transform.

Moving toward win/win is absolutely critical to our species' chance for survival. We have been conditioned to believe in compromise, but compromise is really neither of the parties getting what they want. More than any other factor, the concept of compromise has "gridlocked" our federal government, our business environment, and our social structure and kept us from constructing ever more functional and liberating frames of references in which we could all win. We have all known that some degree of compromise has been necessary in order to avoid chaos and anarchy, but what we have not known is that our efforts have only delayed what may prove to be the otherwise inevitable collapse of our system by allowing for a protracted continuation of what does not work. When parties do not receive the full extent of what they want, as occurs in a compromise situation, resentment, jealousy, revenge, and defensiveness results, drastically reducing the chance of a win/win in the future. Through our compromises, we move further and further away from having what we want.

System Inertia and Fractals

In order to move toward a win/win worldview, we need to develop a mechanism whereby we can more quickly and more accurately sort through the complexity inherent in our world. Perhaps we can look to science. Recently, there has been some discussion regarding the concept of fractals, reappearing similarities that occur regardless of the scale involved so that something as small as DNA and something as large as a galaxy contain essentially the same intricate structures; the central premise is that there is an underlying order in what otherwise appears to be complete randomness. The implications for using a fractal model in studying system inertia is unbelievably exciting since it may contain dramatic new ways for attacking the problem of unmanageable complexity. Moreover, since system inertia is in fact chaotic, we may be able, through fractal analysis, to identify the underlying order and restructure it to our benefit. Lastly, the irrelevance of scale inherent in fractalism is an extremely noteworthy factor since this implies that if we can fundamentally restructure a smaller system then we can do so for a larger one as well.

In many ways, the shifting of the burden away from the system and to the individual is a fractal undertaking. If we can change people, we can change the system. The patterns in us, if arranged in a way that forms a more viable and productive human organism, can be duplicated in the larger whole; if we can become what we would like to become, then our society will follow in the same basic form.

The concept of fractals can be used practically in the discussion of how to remedy system inertia; here, we should not focus so much on specifics as in the framework that fractalism provides. There are probably thousands of ways that fractalism can be used to lift some of the constraints on people operating within the system; i.e., that certain limiting patterns of behavior can be identified and eliminated so that people can change or change more quickly. Perhaps by creating the environment in which we can more easily recognize where we might go, we will get there faster.

The New Individualism, Increasing Knowledge, and System Inertia

As we have discussed, the world is experiencing a tremendous proliferation of knowledge. The knowledge explosion will change the world in unprecedented and unimaginable ways, and what was once thought to be impossible will become possible and what was once "known" will be seen as an illusion. The knowledge explosion will radically alter our concept of the future and we will be able to theorize in new and exciting ways, creating many fascinating connections in which to see ourselves and the world. Some of these will be scientific and some will be humanistic, but in the aggregate all will feed into each other. The combinative benefit will be extremely synergistic and people will increasingly make macro connections with micro implications. To say that people will benefit is a gross understatement; in all that we do the knowledge we create will not only further our own cause in understanding ourselves, but will also augment our efforts at understanding how we relate to our social structures as well. In effect, the knowledge explosion will afford us a tremendous opportunity to comprehend our place in the universe and will enable us to see more clearly how our position helps to form over time our comprehension of reality; most importantly, we will see and really believe that we are a vital part of the cosmos.

The knowledge explosion is bringing us inextricably closer to ourselves; there is an undeniable linkage between what we know and how much we can know ourselves. If we fail to learn during the upcoming knowledge age, it is because of our fears and other self-imposed limitations. This is why we must direct at least a part of future knowledge toward the liberation of the individual, where we actually create a school of thought specifically designed to assist us in the quest for a knowledge that facilitates a furthering of people. We cannot allow knowledge to progress undirected and devoid of a focus on the human benefit, and we must guard against knowledge for knowledge's sake only. There must be a purpose in knowledge and we must determine it.

In furtherance of this objective, we must consider how to combine the proliferation of knowledge with the new individualism. Part of the function of the new individualism, then, must be to ensure that knowledge serves us, in ways that contribute toward the development of a more complete and capable person. The new individualism must seek to make us our knowledge and to make our knowledge advantageous for our existence; we cannot allow the accumulation of knowledge to be distinct from what we are, to think that somehow people are different than what they know or what they choose to know. What we know reveals much about who we are and even more about where we want to be going, and what we seek to know clarifies what we want to be.

Knowledge, specifically the knowledge of the new individualism, is a direct threat to system inertia since system inertia, in large part, results from ignorance. When we learn about system inertia, we increase our understanding; the sum of our knowledge increases as well and we are no longer as much of a victim of the system as before. As we continue to gain in knowledge, system inertia becomes increasingly intolerable; once we define the full extent of the problem by really seeing it for what it is, we will become less able to make allowances for it. In short, the more purposefully knowledgeable we become, the less we will tolerate a system inertia that constrains the drive for a more meaningful understanding of social processes.

The awareness of system inertia becomes a strong motivation for its elimination. When we stop believing "that its just the way it is" and really start to want to live without unnecessary and unwanted systemic encumbrances, then we can take corrective action. Most importantly, an awareness of system inertia creates the necessary ingredients for a remedial mechanism since this awareness is the first step in the journey toward self-correction. Without this recognition, there is no hope for real change.

The key question is marketing. How do we sell the concept that the system can only be changed if we as people change and that education alone will not suffice? The allure of the new individualism is readily noticeable, but distribution and feedback on a massive and all-inclusive scale is extremely difficult to contrive. There are millions of great ideas that have never become accepted on a wide-scale simply because they lacked coherent and effective marketing plans. The new individualism must have such a plan if we are to overcome system inertia and unleash the full extent of our human capabilities.

Theory into Action

Unfortunately, it appears that most of our experience, at least regarding mass movements, has largely demonstrated that theory stays theory and that action is largely inaction. And although many significant trends are already taking shape that feed into the new individualism, there is no guarantee that it will prove universally applicable or arrive in time.

Interestingly, there is a measurement regarding acceptance and universality, expertly discussed and expounded upon in *The Great Boom Ahead* by Harry S. Dent, Jr., known as the "S" curve. The "S" curve is depicted below:

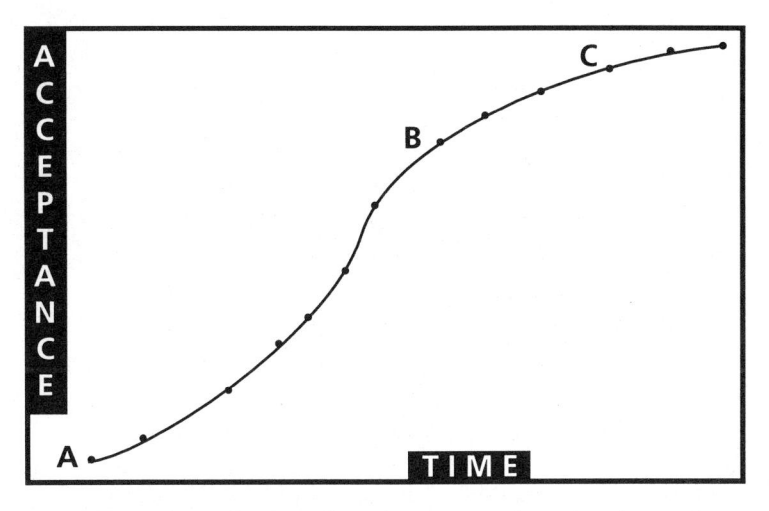

Although used primarily in business and economics to demonstrate product acceptance over time, we can utilize the "S" curve for the acceptance of ideas as well. In our graph, we can see that in the early years of an idea there is virtually no acceptance, point A, but that as time passes, more people begin to accept the idea, point B. Eventually, assuming the idea has widespread applicability, point C is reached where almost near universality is achieved. As more time passes, the acceptance gains past point C are marginal and the idea has essentially run its course. Mr. Dent does a great job, again with products as opposed to ideas, of demonstrating that not all "S" curves are the same shape or take the same amount of time per level of acceptance; moreover, not all products or ideas reach near universality and the degree to which a product or idea is accepted can range from zero to near universality.

Near universality, such as occurred with the automobile, is difficult to achieve but also clearly possible. To be sure, there is an "S" curve on the acceptance of ideas within any specific culture, although the quantification of ideas is a far more difficult undertaking contrasted to the relatively finite measurements like the number of automobiles in a society. In any case, human liberation has an historically very long "S" curve and it will be interesting to see if it ever achieves near universality.

To expedite acceptance, we as a culture have placed much hope on education as the vehicle for widespread social assimilation; this was especially true for the social reform movement of the 1960s. But has education worked? By educating as many Americans as possible, have we achieved our social reformation goals? By educating ourselves and the world through our example, have we forwarded true self-responsibility?

Education has been grounded on the premise that "converts" would become educators themselves and that this conversion process would eventually reach a point of critical mass that would transform society. But, unfortunately, even our much heralded educational efforts have produced ambivalent results and as a result it becomes highly suspect, even idealistic and naive, to expect that education alone can inspire within people the requisite amount of the new individualism.

SYNTHESIS

We cannot make the mistake of entrusting the movement toward real individual responsibility to education alone; we, as a society, have tended to throw virtually all unsolvable problems into the basket of "education" as a way of convenient storage so that we feel we are not actually giving up on them. In effect, we place such problems in limbo, not exactly ready to dismiss them, but certainly not ready to address marketing them. This "storage" appeases our consciences and simultaneously eliminates our guilt. Sadly, through the failure of an almost exclusive reliance on education, we contribute toward the continuation of a system that does not self-correct; in short, the singular reliance on education increases system inertia.

If education alone is not the solution, what is? What must we do to ensure that the new individualism becomes the standard for human behavior? What other options do we have in addition to education? How can we accelerate the "S" curve of the new individualism or ensure that it reaches near universality?

Given the nature of the new individualism and its fundamental belief in the freedom of choice, it is not an option to force or otherwise coerce people into an acceptance of its tenets. Control runs counter to the basic principles of the new individualism. No, we must look at other alternatives that serve to create the proper environment for people to see the beauty and benefit of such a framework.

One option that we have is to actually legislate freedom and self-responsibility; this is what the Constitution and the Bill of Rights are all about anyway. We have made the mistake of legislating in the "interests" of people, but yet most of our laws and regulations are encumbrances upon the drive for self-determination. We need to write into law that people have choice and must exercise self-responsibility because there is no "other" to make these choices for them. This is not coercion, but rather an acceptance of reality. We must legislate against our form of representative democracy and mandate by law participatory democracy; everyone must be involved as a right of citizenship. This is not an infringement on people's right to abstain from voting, but is rather a standard of performance as we have in business or in lawful codes of behavior. Responsibility is a two-way street, toward oneself and toward one's society and as a result reason mandates participation.

Next, we must change the educational process to focus more on self-responsibility and the training necessary to achieve this state of being. We cannot teach "subjects" that promote the belief in external directedness; we need classes that emphasize the choice inherent in living and we need classes that teach that people must be individually responsible if the society is to succeed. We must instruct students on the belief in the possible and we must teach them to focus on process and alternatives.

We also have to pay for our change in education. We must absorb short term debt for long term reward, and we must make certain that the money is spent only on programs that will work; we need measuring systems and an improved forecasting ability to know the feasibility of these programs ahead of time. We must ensure that students recognize that education is a process whereby people learn to be individually responsible for themselves and for the species, and not something one does to make parents happy or to get a job; the value of each individual life must be seen as exceeding the intrinsic value for the holder of that life (his/her life as personally rewarding) and must also be exalted for its relationship to the rest of humanity.

Finally, we need to develop a method whereby we teach self-leadership and not the leading of others. Leadership classes, typical of our external directedness framework, are still taught with the emphasis on how to lead people into missions and assignments which they fail to take on themselves. What about teaching someone how to become a leader of the self? If everyone could lead their own lives, we would no longer require leaders to lead them. The whole idea of separation of people through inequalities as a hierarchical justification has to be trampled; although certainly there are divisions in individual abilities, we do not have to reinforce the perception that this divergence makes a difference in individual worth. If we do not elevate the average, the exceptional will be overcome.

We must also be wary of "comfort traps," those recurring patterns which seem to indicate that our most pressing problems have diminished and which produce complacency or a false sense of security. The most notorious of these is economic prosperity, to which we are now especially vulnerable given the length of the early 1990s recession. A return to prosperity will provide the false perception that our problems have been solved; in reality, it only feels that way and the underlying difficulties will continue unabated, even intensifying, being subject to longer-term cycles and historical trends than that of a business recovery. Because we have been conditioned to believe that economic revival "cures" our social ills, we will lose some of the urgency to fix our current malaise.

There are rational explanations for why things are happening, sometimes we just do not see them. The people who have the greatest impact, because of timing or circumstance, must take it upon themselves to learn and to continue to learn, to really see and know these connections, all the while pushing the boundaries of their own knowledge and wills. The new individualism is not so much a cure as it is a healthful process, wherein people create through their individual unfolding their own creative solutions; by doing so, they keep themselves healthy and well-positioned for their futures through a belief in possibility, not perfection.

Idealism versus Reality

Much of this book has certainly been "urgent," some might even say alarmist, in that much of our sociological dysfunction threatens in a very elementary way the continuation of our species; again, this is not a danger that may be realized for many thousands or even millions of years, but it is nevertheless a distinct possibility. It is preferable to see the message of this book as more one of cautious optimism, more of hopeful probabilities than of apprehension. As discussed throughout, however, it is not etched in stone that we will succeed in our efforts to transform society through personal change, nor is it certain that, as a society, we will even try. The onus is upon us and the outcome is most assuredly uncertain.

As a result, everyone must ask themselves if the odds of success are sufficiently high as to warrant an effort given the threat. For some, myself included, there is no other option except to try because we deserve so much more than we have. For many others, however, the choice toward individual responsibility may not be made until the new individualism has become "the wave." For still others, the choice may be too terrifying and they will instead offer resistance and opposition.

The goal must be to incorporate people through the beauty of a mutually constructed vision that co-destines the fate of the human family with that of all of its members. We must anticipate people's fear and their hesitancy to adopt new ideas, even beneficial ones, and we must know in advance that many people will be unable to push through their insecurities. We must ask ourselves if the passion that once burned in us for reform is still with us or whether the events of the past have tarnished our cultural perception to the point that only apathy remains. We must also seek to be realistic, to pursue a goal that is truly attainable and we must develop feasible strategies to meet that goal. We must draw that fine line between ambition and limitation, to know what can and cannot be done.

To dream is a good thing, but to delude is not. We must be open-minded ourselves, open to criticism by others because the new individualism is formed by all and thus by definition is subject to the changing wills of people over time. We must have confidence that the progression of reason will lead us toward a benevolent commonality and that disputes are nothing more than a chance to reform and perfect our vision.

To accept reality and rid ourselves of illusory influence is one of the great challenges of our time. If we continue to ignore, through our fear and ignorance, the problems of our species we are simply reconciling ourselves to a system inertia that inexorably ensnares us and that eventually collapses back on itself; everything which it has caught will be destroyed. Someday we must pay the price. If we start now, we have a much greater chance of meeting with success.

The Challenge

The beauty of this book is that someone so average wrote it. If someone like myself can see the vast array of social problems confronting our future, then surely experts in a variety of fields must be aware of the same. Many have warned of the dangers inherent in the current global situation and cite our relative inability to do anything about it, and some, like Marilyn Ferguson in *The Aquarian Conspiracy*, recognize the precariousness of today and are nevertheless optimistic that we are indeed busting old paradigms and moving forward into a brighter future.

Certainly, there are people who are in much better positions than myself to recommend remedies to our social ills. Deference to these experts is not the same as external directedness, it is merely the recognition of specific gifts. But the experts must change their perspective, utilizing their abilities with the urgency of the day and with an inclusionary vision for all. This book is really a challenge to knowledgeable people to ask why there is not more being done to advance the human cause and why system inertia is so entrenched. This book is more about structures than about answers to specific problems and an acceptance of choice and self-responsibility is merely a framework that more realistically increases the probability of actual solutions.

THE NEW INDIVIDUALISM

We all need to ask why. We must seek the answer as to why the failures of our system are perpetuated through the generations and why our system is so burdened with personal and social inertia. Moreover, we must find a way to stop the growth of our disinclination to try new things. The new individualism is as much an adaptation as it is an innovation; the system of reliance on others, even our most cherished and revered leaders, has simply not worked. We cannot ask others to do a task that ultimately we must do for ourselves and we cannot expect the system to reform itself without our individual efforts, every single one of us.

The experts and leaders of the world must embrace the new individualism for what it means for people; fear, hierarchies, and external-directedness will certainly endure for many years, but we cannot triumph, as a species, until our experts and leaders understand that our current worldview has been extremely limiting; moreover, they must also understand that victory lies in the empowerment and the elevation of all. We must smash the sanctity of perceived elitism. We must move toward a worldview that is in the interests of all, toward a belief that all are esteemed. We can no longer afford to "lip-service" people, with catch-alls like equality, human rights, and the pursuit of life, liberty, and happiness until we really mean it.

This book is certainly incomplete and intentionally so; people must complete the story. We must all be open, open to the possibility that something better can exist than what exists today. We are conservative to a fault, and we must move beyond our fears and into the realm of the possible. We must incorporate ourselves into the global equation and we must see that we are not predestined to achieve anything other than what we make. We will ultimately be the masters of our own fate, and understandably this is scary. But we must not shy away from this responsibility to self and planet because of our fear and insecurity. We must succeed so that we can pass to successive generations the same opportunities and responsibilities that we have so that the future can be even more promising than how it appears today; that is the way that we would like it, for every successive generation to be an improvement on its predecessor. We deserve to understand our place in the universe and to live more exciting lives. We also deserve to create for ourselves our own morality and the moral structure of our society. Most of all, we deserve to live powerfully, confident in our own abilities and in the possibilities for our future.

About the Author

RICHARD BOTELHO, a native of Danville, California, earned his B.A. and M.A. degrees in Government at California State University, Sacramento. He is employed as a marketing consultant in northern California, where he has worked with a variety of innovative and visionary companies that emphasize personal responsibility as the key to an improved business environment. He has taken much of this model and extrapolated up to the societal level in *The New Individualism*. In addition, he is active in The Executive Committee (TEC) and does substantial public speaking for a variety of organizations, as well as writing articles of widespread consumer interest.

In order for society to advance into a more promising future, we will need to become better people. We simply cannot expect society to somehow transform itself without everyone's improvement. As author Richard Botelho discusses in this seminal work, *The New Individualism: Personal Change to Transform Society*, this will not be an easy task. Noting the disjointed nature that exists between the individual and a "larger whole," he lays much of the blame for our social dysfunction on the lack of personal responsibility. It is only in remedying our individual shortcomings, he writes, that we can even begin to assuage the societal ills that plague us.

In *The New Individualism*, the author identifies the mechanisms that surround and all to often overwhelm the individual: the fears, illusions, insecurities, and lack of sociological promise to which we are all heirs. At the same time, he asserts his belief in the power of people to set things right. By first changing ourselves, we can then hope to significantly alter the world in which we live, a world that will be both more productive and fulfilling.

ORDER FORM

Telephone orders: Call (510) 743-9251

Postal orders: Windstream Publishing Co.
Richard Botelho
303 Windstream Place
Danville, CA 94526

Please send me:

The New Individualism   Copies
  ☐ ISBN 0-9643926-1-5 Hardcover $19.95   _____
  ☐ ISBN 0-9643926-2-3 Softcover $12.95   _____

  ☐ Information on Upcoming Titles

Sales Tax: Please add 7.75% for books shipped to California addresses

Shipping:
  Book Rate $2.00 for the first book and .75 for each additional book.

  Air Mail: $3.50 per book

Payment Method: ☐ Check   ☐ C.O.D.

DOWNTOWN CAMPUS LRC

J. SARGEANT REYNOLDS COMMUNITY COLLEGE
3 7219 001 050 429

HM 136 .B598 1994
Botelho, Richard.
The new individualism

DISCARDED

J. SARGEANT REYNOLDS COMMUNITY COLLEGE
Richmond, VA